# RECIPE ROAD TRIP

# RECIPE ROAD TRIP

## Cooking Your Way Across the USA

**NANETTE LAVIN**

**ILLUSTRATIONS BY KATE EROSHINA**

KITCHEN INK PUBLISHING
NEW YORK

Having fun, making memories in the kitchen, and creating a delicious meal is what KITCHEN INK is all about. Our easy-to-follow, creative, and delicious recipes—kid-tested and parent-approved—include both healthy meals and special treats. Adult supervision and safety first are always important in the Kitchen.

Copyright © 2023 by Kitchen Ink Publishing
www.kitcheninkpublishing.com

Kitchen Ink books are distributed by IPG:
Independent Publishers Group
814 North Franklin Street
Chicago, IL 60610
www.ipgbook.com

Text by Nanette Lavin
Illustrations by Kate Eroshina
Maps by Tanya Keiko

All rights reserved. No part of this publication may be reproduced, distributed, or transmitted in any form or by any means, including photocopying, recording, or other electronic or mechanical methods, without the prior written permission of the publisher, except in the case of brief quotations embodied in critical articles and reviews. For information, address Kitchen Ink Subsidiary Rights Department, 114 John Street, #277, New York, NY 10038.

Produced by Wilsted & Taylor Publishing Services
Copy editing by Melody Lacina
Design and composition by Nancy Koerner
Proofreading by Sophia Fox

Library of Congress Cataloging-in-Publication data is available.
ISBN 978-1-943016-14-3

First Edition
27 26 25 24     10 9 8 7 6 5 4 3 2

KITCHEN INK PUBLISHING
NEW YORK

Kitchen Ink books may be purchased for educational, business, or sales promotional use. For information, please email the Special Markets Department at sales@kitcheninkpublishing.com.

  See what Kitchen Ink is up to, share recipes and tips, and shop our store—www.kitcheninkpublishing.com.

To my husband, Jimmy, a man who loved a good meal and an even better joke. Your bad "dad jokes," puns, and one-liners are missed almost as much as you are.

To my daughter, Emma, who inspires me with her kind, caring nature. You are my pride and joy, and your cooking isn't so bad, either!

# CONTENTS

About *Recipe Road Trip* . . . xiii

## NORTHEAST . . . 1

### Connecticut
Soft Pumpkin Cookies . . . **2**
Cheeseburgers in Puff Pastry . . . **3**

### Delaware
Strawberry Smoothie . . . **5**
Peach Pie . . . **6**

### Maine
Lobster Rolls . . . **8**
Mini Whoopie Pies . . . **9**

### Maryland
Crab Cakes . . . **11**
Berger Cookies . . . **12**

### Massachusetts
Boston Baked Beans . . . **14**
Mini Boston Cream Pie . . . **15**

### New Hampshire
Apple Cider Doughnuts . . . **18**
New Hampshire Corn Chowder . . . **20**

### New Jersey
Salt Water Taffy . . . **21**
Green Bean Salad . . . **22**

### New York
Red Velvet Cake . . . **23**
Waldorf Salad . . . **25**

### Pennsylvania
Philly Cheesesteak . . . **26**
Soft Pretzels . . . **27**

### Rhode Island
Frozen Lemonade . . . **29**
Johnny Cakes . . . **30**

### Vermont
Maple Candy . . . **31**
Macaroni and Cheese . . . **32**

# SOUTHEAST ... 35

## Alabama
Oven Fried Green Tomatoes ... 36
Pecan Pie Mini Muffins ... 37

## Arkansas
Fried Pickles ... 38
Arkansas Rice Casserole ... 39

## Florida
Key Lime Pie ... 40
Sunburst Drink ... 41

## Georgia
No-Bake Peanut Butter Pie ... 42
Southern Fried Chicken ... 43

## Kentucky
Hot Brown Sandwiches ... 45
Kentucky Derby Pie ... 47

## Louisiana
Easy King Cake ... 48
Yeti Baked Alaska ... 49
Fondant ... 51

## Mississippi
Mississippi Mud Pie ... 52
Pimento Cheese ... 55

## North Carolina
Sweet Potato Balls ... 56
Creamy Coleslaw ... 57

## South Carolina
Shrimp and Grits ... 58
Frogmore Stew ... 59

## Tennessee
Nashville Hot Chicken ... 60
Banana Pudding ... 62

## Virginia
Boiled Peanuts ... 63
Ham and Cheese Biscuits ... 64

## West Virginia
Pepperoni Rolls ... 66
Skillet Cornbread ... 68
Honey Butter ... 69

# MIDWEST . . . 71

## Illinois
Chicago-Style Pizza . . . 72
Chicago-Style Hot Dog . . . 74

## Indiana
Classic Pork Tenderloin Sandwiches . . . 75
Sugar Cream Pie . . . 77

## Iowa
Sweet and Easy Corn on the Cob . . . 79
Egg and Sweet Corn Frittata . . . 80

## Kansas
Brown Sugar Oat Muffins . . . 81
Wholesome Wheat Bread . . . 82

## Michigan
Cherry Salad . . . 83
Cherry Pie . . . 84

## Minnesota
Minnesota Hot Dish Casserole . . . 85
Blueberry Muffins . . . 86

## Missouri
Fried Ravioli . . . 87
Ozark Sloppy Joes . . . 88

## Nebraska
Classic Reuben Sandwiches . . . 89
Corn Fritters . . . 90

## North Dakota
Chippers (Chocolate-Covered Potato Chips) . . . 91
Honey Vanilla French Toast . . . 92

## Ohio
Buckeyes . . . 93
Authentic Cincinnati Chili . . . 94

## South Dakota
Kuchen . . . 96
Oven-Roasted Vegetables . . . 97

## Wisconsin
Cheese Fondue . . . 98
Wisconsin Cheese Soup . . . 99

# SOUTHWEST ... 101

## Arizona
Baked Chicken Chimichangas ... **102**
Breakfast Burritos with Avocado-Tomato Salsa ... **103**

## New Mexico
Guacamole ... **105**
Huevos Rancheros ... **106**

## Oklahoma
Chicken-Fried Steak ... **108**
Oklahoma Cheese Grits ... **109**

## Texas
Slow Cooker Texas Pulled Pork ... **110**
Country Potato Salad ... **111**

# WEST ... 113

## Alaska
Salmon Croquettes ... **114**
Blueberry Meringue Pie ... **115**

## California
Avocado Toast ... **117**
Fish Tacos ... **118**

## Colorado
Denver Omelet ... **120**
Watermelon Sorbet ... **121**

## Hawaii
Roasted Pineapple Salsa ... **122**
Spam Fries ... **123**

## Idaho
Huckleberry Pop Tarts ... **124**
Idaho Fries ... **126**

## Montana
Wheat Cinnamon Rolls ... **127**
Beef Pasties ... **129**

## Nevada
Onion Rings ... **132**
Shrimp Cocktail ... **133**

## Oregon
Blueberry Hazelnut Breakfast Cookies ... **134**
Almond Butter and Nut Pear Wedges ... **135**

## Utah
Pineapple Cucumber Lime Jell-O Salad . . . **136**
Potato Casserole . . . **137**

## Washington
Wild Mushroom Barley . . . **138**
Emma's Applesauce . . . **139**

## Wyoming
Wyoming Stew . . . **140**
Wyoming Cowboy Cookies . . . **141**

# THE FEDERAL DISTRICT, AMERICAN COMMONWEALTHS, AND TERRITORIES . . . **143**

## Washington, D.C.
Senate Bean Soup . . . **144**
Mambo Sauce . . . **145**

## Puerto Rico
Empanadillas (Puerto Rican Fried Turnovers) . . . **146**
Sofrito . . . **147**
Tostones (Fried Green Plantains) . . . **148**
Mojo Verde . . . **149**

## Northern Marianas Islands
Coconut Rice . . . **150**
Rosketti . . . **151**

## Guam
Buñelos Aga (Banana Doughnuts) . . . **153**
Cucumber Salad . . . **154**

## American Samoa
Palusami . . . **155**
Samoan Poi . . . **156**

## US Virgin Islands
Fungi . . . **157**
Callaloo . . . **159**

# MENUS ... 161

## Northeast Menu

Waldorf Salad ... **164**
Boston Baked Beans ... **165**
Corned Beef and Cabbage ... **166**
Mini Whoopie Pies ... **168**

## Southeast Menu

Creamy Coleslaw ... **172**
Sweet and Easy Corn
 on the Cob ... **173**
Southern Fried Chicken ... **174**
Key Lime Pie ... **176**

## Midwest Menu

Wisconsin Cheese Soup ... **178**
Broccoli Casserole ... **179**
Scalloped Potatoes ... **180**
Meatloaf ... **181**
Cherry Pie ... **182**

## Southwest Menu

Guacamole ... **184**
Southwestern Rice ... **185**
Chicken Enchiladas ... **186**
Enchilada Sauce ... **187**
Mango Pineapple Sorbet
 with Honey ... **188**

## West Menu

Country Potato Salad ... **190**
Cowboy Dinner (Cornbread, Beef,
 and Bean Casserole) ... **191**
Wyoming Cowboy Cookies ... **193**

Recipes by Category ... 195
Recipes by Level of Difficulty ... 199
Acknowledgments ... 204
Index ... 205

## About *Recipe Road Trip*

The goal of this book is to educate, entertain, and create delicious food for everyone to enjoy. The recipes included here introduce you to dishes from around the United States. Some reflect the crops grown locally, while others have historical significance. A number of these recipes reflect the vast cultural and ethnic backgrounds of the people who reside in this country.

*Recipe Road Trip* was written with the expectation that an adult will be in the kitchen supervising and contributing to the creation of each dish. Recipes have been categorized by level of difficulty. Easier recipes encourage the beginner who is learning to cook, while more difficult recipes expand the kitchen skills of the more experienced learner. Each recipe has a number showing its level of difficulty: 1 for "easy," 2 for "a bit more challenging," and 3 for "more challenging, with multiple steps." If deep frying is included, the recipe is automatically a 3.

Replacement suggestions and cooking tips appear throughout the book. For safety and ease, use an air fryer for deep frying when possible.

This book contains recipes from the fifty states, one federal district, two American commonwealths, and three American territories that constitute the United States. *Recipe Road Trip* will spark any chef in training. While traveling through the USA from your kitchen, you will not only learn how to make delicious food but also learn geography, fun facts, and laugh-out-loud jokes. It is a road trip you will want to take over and over. No suitcase required!

Enjoy!

*Nanette Lavin*

Nanette Lavin

# RECIPE ROAD TRIP

# NORTHEAST

Much of the interior of the Northeast is formed by the Appalachian Mountains, which stretch about 1,600 miles from Maine to Alabama. Some of the region's resources come from underground, like granite, marble, and coal. The Northeast is the nation's most economically developed, densely populated, and culturally diverse area.

## 11 STATES

**Connecticut** . . . 2
**Delaware** . . . 5
**Maine** . . . 8
**Maryland** . . . 11
**Massachusetts** . . . 14
**New Hampshire** . . . 18
**New Jersey** . . . 21
**New York** . . . 23
**Pennsylvania** . . . 26
**Rhode Island** . . . 29
**Vermont** . . . 31

# CONNECTICUT · CT

## Soft Pumpkin Cookies

**LEVEL 2**

*Makes 32 cookies*

### INGREDIENTS

2½ cups all-purpose flour
1 teaspoon baking soda
1 teaspoon baking powder
1 teaspoon ground cinnamon
½ teaspoon ground nutmeg
½ teaspoon salt
1½ cups granulated sugar

½ cup (1 stick)
    plus 1 tablespoon butter, softened
1 cup 100% pure pumpkin
1 large egg
2 teaspoons vanilla extract
2 cups confectioners' sugar, sifted
3 tablespoons milk

### DIRECTIONS

1. Preheat oven to 350°F. Grease or line with parchment paper two 12 × 17-inch baking sheets.
2. In a medium bowl, combine flour, baking soda, baking powder, cinnamon, nutmeg, and salt.
3. In a large bowl, beat sugar and ½ cup butter until well blended. Beat in pumpkin, egg, and 1 teaspoon vanilla extract until smooth. Gradually beat in flour mixture.
4. Drop by rounded tablespoon 2 inches apart onto prepared baking sheets.
5. Bake for 15 to 18 minutes or until edges are firm.
6. Remove from oven and cool on baking sheets for 2 minutes; remove to wire racks to cool completely.
7. Make the glaze: combine sifted confectioners' sugar, milk, remaining tablespoon butter, and remaining teaspoon vanilla extract in small bowl and stir until smooth.
8. Drizzle glaze over cookies.

# CONNECTICUT · CT

## Cheeseburgers in Puff Pastry

**LEVEL 1**

*Makes 4 burgers*

### INGREDIENTS

1 pound ground beef
½ teaspoon lemon and pepper seasoning
½ teaspoon garlic salt
4 slices bacon, cooked
4 cheese slices
4 tomato slices
1 package puff pastry sheets
1 egg white
1 tablespoon water

### DIRECTIONS

1. Pat out 4 hamburgers. Season with lemon and pepper seasoning and garlic salt. Cook burgers your preferred way—grilled, baked, or fried.
2. While burgers are cooking, lay out puff pastry sheets to thaw.
3. After burgers finish cooking, top with cheese slices and set aside.
4. Preheat oven to 400°F. Open pastry sheets and slice into 4 squares. Roll out squares to stretch.
5. Place one burger in the middle of a puff pastry. Top with bacon and tomato.

Home of the first hamburger. Louis Lassen claims he created the first hamburger sandwich at Louie's Lunch in New Haven in 1900.

NORTHEAST 3

# CONNECTICUT · CT

6. Fold ends of puff pastry together to cover burger and then press seams together. The burger will be completely covered by the dough. Continue until all burgers have been covered. Lay them seam side down on a baking sheet.

7. Beat egg white with water. Brush tops of puff pastry burgers with egg wash and then place burgers in oven to bake for 10 to 12 minutes.

8. Remove burgers from oven and serve with ketchup and/or mustard!

*Did you hear about the cheeseburger patty who told funny jokes?*

*He was on a roll.*

# DELAWARE · DE

## Strawberry Smoothie

**LEVEL 1**

*Serves 1*

### INGREDIENTS

2 cups frozen strawberries
1 banana, room temperature and cut into pieces
¼ cup Greek yogurt
1 cup milk, almond milk, or soy milk
1½ tablespoons maple syrup, honey, or agave
½ cup ice

### DIRECTIONS

1. Place strawberries, banana, yogurt, milk, syrup, and ice in a blender.
2. Blend until creamy and frothy, stopping and scraping down the sides as necessary.
3. Pour into a glass and garnish with a strawberry.

# DELAWARE · DE

## Peach Pie

**LEVEL 2**
Serves 8

### INGREDIENTS

3 pounds peaches, sliced
¾ cup sugar
2 tablespoons fresh lemon juice
¾ teaspoon ground cinnamon
4 tablespoons minute tapioca
3 cups all-purpose flour
¾ teaspoon salt
½ cup vegetable shortening
½ cup (1 stick) plus 1 tablespoon chilled butter, cut into pieces
½ cup ice water
1 egg, beaten
1 tablespoon sugar

*Did you hear the joke about the peach? It was pit-iful.*

### DIRECTIONS

1. Preheat oven to 400°F.

2. In a large bowl, combine peaches, sugar, lemon juice, and cinnamon. Stir in 2 tablespoons minute tapioca. Let stand, stirring occasionally.

3. In another large bowl, combine flour and salt. Using a mixer, work in shortening and ½ cup butter until mixture resembles coarse crumbs. Sprinkle 1 tablespoon ice water over flour mixture, stirring gently with a fork. Continue adding water just until dough holds together. Shape dough into a ball and divide it into two disks, one slightly larger than the other.

# DELAWARE · DE

4. Place smaller disk on a sheet of waxed paper, and use a lightly floured rolling pin to roll dough into a 12-inch circle. If dough sticks to the rolling pin, dust it with more flour. Lay a 9- to 10-inch pie pan facedown on top of dough, flip pan over, and remove waxed paper. For the top crust, on a sheet of waxed paper, roll out the other disk to form a 14-inch circle. Do not roll dough more than necessary.

5. Sprinkle rest of minute tapioca on bottom crust. Add peach filling, mounding it in the center, and dot with 1 tablespoon butter. Lift waxed paper with top crust and flip it over the filling. Peel back waxed paper. Trim edges of crusts and pinch together top and bottom crusts. Brush pie with the egg, sprinkle top with sugar, and poke holes to vent. Bake 40 to 45 minutes, or until golden brown. Serve warm.

**Delaware has the largest population of horseshoe crabs in the world. It is estimated that horseshoe crabs predate dinosaurs by more than 200 million years.**

NORTHEAST

# MAINE • ME

## Lobster Rolls

**LEVEL 2**

*Serves 10*

### INGREDIENTS

2 pounds Maine lobster meat, cooked
1 tablespoon fresh dill, chopped
1 tablespoon fresh parsley, chopped
¼ cup mayonnaise
½ teaspoon salt
½ teaspoon garlic powder
¼ teaspoon black pepper
10 New England–style frankfurter rolls
5 tablespoons butter, softened

### DIRECTIONS

1. Drain cooked lobster meat in a colander for 5 minutes. If using claw meat, you do not need to chop it, unless you want smaller pieces. (If using lobster tail, chop it into bite-size pieces.) Move lobster meat to large mixing bowl.

2. Chop fresh herbs. Add to lobster meat, and then add mayonnaise, dill, parsley, salt, garlic powder, and pepper. Mix well.

3. Cover and chill until ready to serve.

4. Spread both flat sides of rolls with a generous amount of butter.

5. Heat a large skillet or griddle to medium heat. Place rolls flat side down in skillet. Toast for 1 to 3 minutes until golden brown. Then flip and toast other side for 1 to 3 minutes. Remove and repeat as needed.

6. Once rolls are perfectly toasted, load them with lobster salad and serve!

*Why don't lobsters share?*
*They are shellfish.*

RECIPE ROAD TRIP

# MAINE · ME

## Mini Whoopie Pies

**LEVEL 2**

*Makes 24 pies*

### INGREDIENTS

2¼ cups all-purpose flour
½ cup unsweetened cocoa powder
1 teaspoon baking soda
2 teaspoons cream of tartar
1 teaspoon salt
⅔ cup vegetable shortening
1¼ cups granulated sugar
2 large eggs
3 teaspoons vanilla extract
1 cup milk
½ cup unsalted butter
1 cup confectioners' sugar
2 cups marshmallow creme

The first known commercially produced whoopie pies were sold in 1925 by Labadie's Bakery in Lewiston. In 2011, the Maine Legislature designated the whoopie pie as Maine's official state treat.

### DIRECTIONS

1. Preheat oven to 350°F. Grease 2 large baking sheets; set aside.

2. In a medium bowl, whisk together flour, cocoa, baking soda, cream of tartar, and salt; set aside.

3. In a large bowl, cream together shortening and granulated sugar. Beat in eggs and 2 teaspoons vanilla extract. Alternately add flour mixture and milk, beating until fully combined.

# MAINE • ME

4. Drop dough by tablespoons 2 inches apart onto prepared baking sheets.

5. Bake for 8 to 10 minutes or until darker around the edges and firm to the touch. Transfer cakes to a wire rack to cool completely.

6. In a medium bowl, beat together butter and confectioners' sugar. Beat in marshmallow creme and remaining teaspoon vanilla extract until smooth.

7. Spoon 1 tablespoon filling onto bottom of a cake. Press bottom of a second cake against filling to make a sandwich. Repeat with remaining cakes and filling.

8. To store, layer whoopie pies between sheets of waxed paper in an airtight container and refrigerate for up to 2 days.

# MARYLAND · MD

## Crab Cakes

**LEVEL 1**

*Makes 6 cakes*

*What is the best job for a crab? A crab driver!*

### INGREDIENTS

- 1 large egg
- ¼ cup mayonnaise
- 1 tablespoon chopped fresh parsley or 2 teaspoons dried
- 2 teaspoons Dijon mustard
- 2 teaspoons Worcestershire sauce
- 1 teaspoon Old Bay® seasoning
- 1 teaspoon fresh lemon juice, plus more for serving
- ⅛ teaspoon salt
- 1 pound fresh lump crab meat
- ⅔ cup saltine cracker crumbs
- 2 tablespoons butter, melted

### DIRECTIONS

1. In a large bowl, whisk egg, mayonnaise, parsley, Dijon mustard, Worcestershire sauce, Old Bay,® lemon juice, and salt. Place crab meat on top, followed by cracker crumbs. With a rubber spatula or large spoon, very gently and carefully fold together. Don't break up crab meat.

2. Cover tightly and refrigerate for at least 30 minutes and up to 1 day.

3. Preheat oven to 450°F. Generously grease a rimmed baking sheet with butter or nonstick spray or line with a silicone baking mat.

4. Portion crab cake mixture into 6 mounds on baking sheet. Use your hands or a spoon to compact mounds so they aren't lumpy or falling apart, but don't flatten them. For extra flavor, brush each with melted butter—this is optional but recommended!

5. Bake for 12 to 14 minutes or until lightly browned around the edges and on top. Drizzle each crab cake with fresh lemon juice and serve warm.

NORTHEAST

# MARYLAND • MD

## Berger Cookies

**LEVEL 2**

*Makes 24 cookies*

### INGREDIENTS

#### COOKIES

5 tablespoons unsalted butter, softened
½ teaspoon salt
1½ teaspoons vanilla extract
½ cup granulated sugar
1 egg
1½ cups all-purpose flour
1 teaspoon baking powder
⅓ cup whole milk

#### FROSTING

½ cup semisweet chocolate chips
½ cup Dutch cocoa powder, sifted
1 teaspoon vanilla extract
⅓ cup heavy cream, plus more as needed
1 cup confectioners' sugar, plus more as needed
⅛ teaspoon salt

### DIRECTIONS

#### COOKIES

1. In a large bowl, combine butter, salt, vanilla extract, and sugar. Add egg and combine well. In another bowl, combine flour and baking powder. Add dry ingredients to wet a little at a time, then slowly stir in milk.
2. Refrigerate dough for 30 minutes. When ready to bake, preheat oven to 400°F.
3. Drop by rounded tablespoons onto a lined baking sheet. Flatten slightly with a flat-bottom cup so that each cookie is 1½ inches across. Leave 2 inches between cookies.
4. Bake for 9 to 11 minutes or until bottoms are golden, while tops remain white. Allow cookies to cool completely before icing.

# MARYLAND · MD

### FROSTING

1. Using a double boiler, melt chocolate chips.
2. In a medium bowl using an electric mixer, combine melted chips, cocoa, and vanilla extract. Blend in cream, confectioners' sugar, and salt.
3. Remove from heat while frosting is still warm (not hot) to finish blending out any remaining lumps. If frosting is too runny, add more powdered sugar. If it's too stiff, add 1 teaspoon cream at a time and blend until you have a thick, fudgy frosting.
4. Frost flat side of each cookie for a black-and-white effect. Refrigerate any uneaten cookies.

*Assateague Island is home of the wild Chincoteague ponies. Today the state park assists the National Park Service in managing the Maryland herd of 155 horses.*

NORTHEAST

# MASSACHUSETTS · MA

## Boston Baked Beans

**LEVEL 2**

*Serves 6 to 8*

### INGREDIENTS

8 ounces bacon (7 to 8 slices), cut into ½-inch pieces
1 medium onion, finely chopped
5 garlic cloves, minced
2 tablespoons brown sugar
⅓ cup molasses
One 15-ounce can diced tomatoes
⅓ cup ketchup
2 tablespoons Worcestershire sauce
2 tablespoons yellow mustard
2 teaspoons paprika
2 bay leaves
½ teaspoon black pepper
½ teaspoon cloves, ground
1 teaspoon kosher salt
Three 15-ounce cans navy beans, drained

### DIRECTIONS

1. Preheat oven to 325°F.
2. Heat a 6-quart Dutch oven over medium heat. Add bacon and cook until crisp and fat is rendered, 7 to 10 minutes. Transfer bacon to a bowl using a slotted spoon.
3. Add onions and garlic to bacon fat in pot and sauté until soft and translucent, about 5 minutes. Add brown sugar, molasses, tomatoes, ketchup, Worcestershire sauce, mustard, paprika, bay leaves, pepper, cloves, salt, navy beans, and reserved bacon to the pot.
4. Over medium-high heat, bring mixture to a simmer, stirring frequently. Cover pot with lid and transfer to the oven. Bake until sauce has thickened, 45 to 55 minutes. Check beans and stir once halfway through cooking time.
5. Let beans rest out of the oven for 10 minutes before serving. Garnish with extra bacon if desired.

# MASSACHUSETTS · MA

## Mini Boston Cream Pie

**LEVEL 3**
*Serves 6 to 8*

> Why were the pirates happy when they washed up to shore and saw cakes, ice cream, and pie? It was a desserted island.

### INGREDIENTS

#### CREAM FILLING

1 large egg yolk
2 tablespoons sugar
2 teaspoons cornstarch
½ cup whole milk
½ tablespoon salted butter
¼ teaspoon vanilla extract

#### CAKE

4 tablespoons salted butter, melted
5 tablespoons sugar
2 large egg whites
1 teaspoon vanilla extract
½ cup self-rising flour
¼ cup heavy cream

#### CHOCOLATE GANACHE

¼ cup semisweet chocolate chips
¼ cup heavy cream

### DIRECTIONS

#### CREAM FILLING

1. In a small bowl, whisk egg yolk and then set bowl aside.
2. In a saucepan, add sugar, cornstarch, and milk and stir until smooth.
3. Place saucepan over medium heat and cook, whisking constantly until mixture begins to thicken and bubble. Continue to cook while whisking for 1 additional minute.
4. In a medium bowl, add egg and slowly add milk mixture 1 teaspoon at a time, whisking constantly, until all milk has been added.

# MASSACHUSETTS · MA

5. Pour egg mixture back into saucepan and bring to a simmer. Cook over medium-high heat for 1 minute, stirring frequently.

6. Remove from heat and stir in butter and vanilla extract. Continue to stir until smooth. Transfer to a bowl, cover, and refrigerate until you are ready to use.

### CAKE

1. Preheat oven to 350°F. Lightly grease two 10-ounce ramekins.

2. In a medium bowl, using a mixer on medium speed, beat butter, sugar, egg whites, and vanilla extract until smooth.

3. Add self-rising flour and mix for a few seconds, until flour is just mixed in.

4. Add cream and mix until smooth.

5. Divide batter evenly between prepared ramekins.

6. Bake for 20 to 25 minutes or until a toothpick inserted in the center of each cake comes out clean.

7. Cool cakes completely on a wire rack. As cakes cool, remove cream filling from refrigerator. The cream should be room temperature, for ease of spreading.

8. Once cakes are cool, run a thin knife around edges to release cakes from ramekins. If your mini cake layers bake up with domed tops, simply use a long, sharp knife to slice off tops. Leveling off the tops is optional, but it gives the cream filling and second cake layer a flat surface to rest on.

**Not only did the Omni Parker House create the delicious Boston cream pie in 1856, but the hotel's restaurant still serves the original version today.**

# MASSACHUSETTS · MA

### CHOCOLATE GANACHE

1. Place chocolate chips in a small bowl.
2. Heat heavy cream in a 1-quart saucepan over medium-low heat until cream begins to gently simmer. Alternatively, heat it in the microwave in a microwave-safe bowl until it starts to bubble; watch it carefully so it does not boil over.
3. Pour hot cream over chocolate chips and let sit for 2 to 3 minutes. This rest time allows the hot cream to melt the chocolate while at the same time brings down the temperature of the cream. If you whisk while the cream is still hot, the ganache could break down, resulting in a gritty texture.
4. After chocolate has had enough time to melt, stir cream and chocolate together slowly.

### ASSEMBLY

1. Place one layer of cake on a serving plate.
2. Spread cream filling over cake.
3. Top with the second cake layer and gently press down.
4. Pour ganache over the top of the cake and spread to the edges.
5. Refrigerate the cake until firm enough to slice, which will take at least 1 hour.

**NOTE** Why is it called a pie when it's a cake? In the mid-nineteenth century, pie tins were more common than cake pans. The first versions of this recipe were baked in pie tins. Boston cream pie is a remake of the early American pudding-cake pie.

NORTHEAST

# NEW HAMPSHIRE • NH

## Apple Cider Doughnuts

**LEVEL 3**

*Makes 20 doughnuts*

### INGREDIENTS

1 cup apple cider
4½ cups all-purpose flour
1 tablespoon baking powder
1 teaspoon baking soda
1 teaspoon kosher salt
2 teaspoons ground cinnamon
½ teaspoon ground nutmeg
½ cup granulated sugar
½ cup firmly packed brown sugar
6 tablespoons unsalted butter, softened
2 large eggs, room temperature
½ cup buttermilk
1 teaspoon vanilla extract
1 medium Macoun or Macintosh apple, peeled, cored, and grated
Canola oil for frying

### CINNAMON SUGAR

1½ cups granulated sugar
2–3 tablespoons ground cinnamon
1 teaspoon ground nutmeg

### DIRECTIONS

1. In a medium saucepan over low heat, reduce apple cider to about ¾ cup, about 30 minutes. Set aside and cool to room temperature.

2. In a medium bowl, sift together flour, baking powder, baking soda, salt, cinnamon, and nutmeg and set aside.

3. In a large bowl, using an electric mixer, cream together granulated sugar, brown sugar, and butter.

4. Add eggs one at a time and continue to mix until incorporated. Use a rubber spatula to occasionally scrape sides and bottom of bowl.

5. Add apple cider, buttermilk, and vanilla extract, mixing to combine. Add flour mixture and combine.

RECIPE ROAD TRIP

# NEW HAMPSHIRE · NH

6. Gently fold grated apples into batter.

7. Line a baking sheet with parchment paper and set aside.

8. Turn dough out onto a well-floured flat surface. This dough can be sticky. Use a silicone spatula to fold dough over and flour before cutting doughnuts.

9. Use a rolling pin to roll out the dough to ½-inch thickness. Lightly flour a doughnut cutter and cut out doughnuts, placing them on prepared baking sheet as you work.

10. Line another baking sheet with several layers of paper towels and set aside.

11. In a large, heavy pot, pour about 3 inches of canola oil. Heat to 375°F. Drop about 4 to 5 doughnuts into oil, making sure not to overcrowd the pot. Cook for 1 to 2 minutes on each side, or until lightly golden brown.

12. Remove doughnuts from oil and allow to drain on paper towels.

13. In a small bowl, combine all ingredients for cinnamon sugar; mix well.

14. While doughnuts are still warm, sprinkle with cinnamon sugar.

**TIP** If you don't own a doughnut cutter, clean a can from canned vegetables. The sharp, thin edge of the opened can will cut through the dough, and finding a small, circular object to cut the doughnut's center hole should be easy.

NORTHEAST 19

# NEW HAMPSHIRE · NH

## New Hampshire Corn Chowder

**LEVEL 2**

Serves 6

### INGREDIENTS

2 tablespoons butter
1 onion, chopped
½ cup diced celery
6 tablespoons all-purpose flour
Two 14.5-ounce cans vegetable broth
Two 14.5-ounce cans creamed corn
One 15-ounce can whole-kernel corn, drained

2 tablespoons shredded carrot
1 cup half-and-half
¾ cup skim milk
¼ teaspoon ground nutmeg
¼ teaspoon ground black pepper
¼ teaspoon salt

### DIRECTIONS

1. In a large saucepan over medium heat, melt butter. Add onions and celery, cooking 3 minutes.

2. Whisk in flour and cook 6 minutes more, until light brown. Whisk in broth and simmer 10 minutes.

3. Stir in creamed corn, corn, carrot, half-and-half, milk, nutmeg, pepper, and salt. Simmer over low heat 10 minutes more.

*The first American alarm clock was created in 1787 by Levi Hutchins in Concord, New Hampshire.*

# NEW JERSEY • NJ

## Salt Water Taffy

**LEVEL 2**
*Makes 30 pieces*

### INGREDIENTS

½ cup granulated sugar
½ tablespoon corn starch
⅓ cup light corn syrup
½ tablespoon unsalted butter, plus more for greasing

¼ cup water
¼ teaspoon salt
¼ teaspoon extract of choice (optional)
1–2 drops of food coloring (optional)

### DIRECTIONS

1. Generously grease a standard 8 × 8-inch baking pan and set aside.
2. In a small or medium-sized saucepan, heat sugar, corn starch, corn syrup, butter, water, and salt on medium-high heat until bubbles form. Keep stirring until mixture reaches 250°F.
3. Remove saucepan from heat and add extract and food coloring if using. Pour mixture into greased baking pan. Using a well-buttered bench scraper, fold mixture onto itself until it is cool enough to touch.
4. Generously butter your hands and stretch candy into a long rope. Fold it in half so ends meet, and stretch again. Repeat for about 5 to 10 minutes or until candy gets lighter and lighter in color.
5. Finally, pull candy into a rope about ½ inch wide (or whatever thickness you'd like). Set it down and, using a well-buttered pair of scissors, cut into small pieces.
6. Allow candy to rest for about 30 minutes before wrapping in parchment paper or waxed paper.

# NEW JERSEY • NJ

## Green Bean Salad

**LEVEL 1**

*Serves 6*

### INGREDIENTS

1 pound green beans, ends trimmed
1 small red onion, minced
1 tablespoon red wine vinegar
¼ teaspoon fine sea salt
¼ teaspoon sugar
⅛ teaspoon dry mustard
3 tablespoons olive oil

### DIRECTIONS

1. Prepare a large bowl of ice water and set aside.
2. Place beans in a microwave-safe container with 2 tablespoons water. Microwave at 1-minute intervals until desired temperature is reached.
3. Once beans are steamed, immediately plunge them in the ice water. Swish beans around until completely cool. Dry thoroughly. Put dried green beans in a shallow dish.
4. In a small bowl, combine onion, vinegar, and salt.
5. Whisk sugar, dry mustard, and oil into onion mixture.
6. Pour dressing over green beans, toss beans to coat with dressing, cover the container, and chill at least 1 hour and up to overnight.

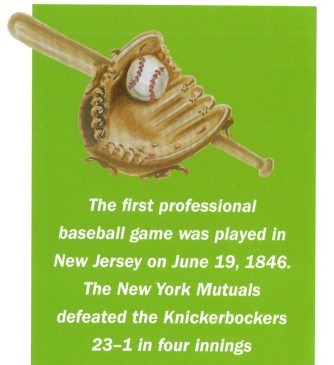

*The first professional baseball game was played in New Jersey on June 19, 1846. The New York Mutuals defeated the Knickerbockers 23–1 in four innings at Elysian Fields.*

*What veggie can tie your stomach in knots?*
*A string bean.*

RECIPE ROAD TRIP

# NEW YORK • NY

## Red Velvet Cake

**LEVEL 3**

*Serves 8*

### INGREDIENTS

#### CAKE

2½ cups all-purpose flour

1 teaspoon salt

1 teaspoon baking soda

½ cup unsalted butter, room temperature

1½ cups granulated sugar

2 large eggs, room temperature

2 teaspoons vanilla extract

2 tablespoons cocoa powder

1 cup buttermilk, room temperature

1 tablespoon white vinegar

1–2 tablespoons liquid red food coloring

**TIP** This recipe can be modified to make cupcakes, a Bundt cake, or two cake layers instead of three.

#### CREAM CHEESE FROSTING

Two 8-ounce blocks cream cheese, room temperature

1½ cups unsalted butter, room temperature

1 teaspoon vanilla extract

Pinch kosher salt

5½ cups confectioners' sugar, sifted

### DIRECTIONS

#### CAKE

1. Preheat oven to 350°F. Butter and flour three 6-inch cake pans.

2. In a medium bowl, sift together flour, salt, and baking soda.

3. In a large bowl, using an electric mixer, cream butter on medium speed. Add in sugar and mix on medium until light and fluffy, about 3 minutes. Add in eggs one at a time, beating each until well combined. Beat in vanilla extract.

4. Sift cocoa powder into butter mixture and beat just until combined. Scrape down the bowl.

# NEW YORK • NY

5. In a liquid measuring cup, mix buttermilk, vinegar, and red food coloring.

6. With mixer on low speed, add half of flour mixture followed by half of buttermilk mixture to the mixing bowl, beating just until combined. Repeat with remaining flour and buttermilk. Stop and scrape down the bowl occasionally. Divide batter among prepared pans.

7. Bake for about 30 to 35 minutes or until centers are springy to the touch. When done, let cake layers cool in their pans for about 10 minutes, and then turn them out onto a wire rack to cool completely.

### FROSTING

1. In a large mixing bowl, beat cream cheese and butter together on medium speed until smooth and fluffy, about 3 minutes.

2. Add vanilla extract and salt and beat until combined.

3. Sift confectioners' sugar into a large bowl.

4. With mixer on low speed, gradually add sugar into butter mixture, scraping down the bowl occasionally. Increase speed to medium and beat until fluffy, about 1 minute. Place about a cup of frosting in a piping bag with a decorative tip.

### ASSEMBLY

1. For three layers, place a cake layer on a cake stand or serving plate. Spread about ½ cup frosting on top of cake. Place another layer on top and frost it. Top with final cake layer and spread remaining frosting all over top and sides of cake. Use a spatula to smooth out frosting. Pipe a decorative border on top of cake or as desired. Chill cake for about 1 hour or until frosting is set.

2. If making cupcakes or a Bundt cake, allow time to cool prior to frosting.

# NEW YORK • NY

## Waldorf Salad

**LEVEL 1**

Serves 2

### INGREDIENTS

2 large Gala or Honeycrisp apples, unpeeled and chopped
2 cups chopped celery
¼ cup raisins
¼ cup walnuts, toasted
⅓ cup reduced-fat mayonnaise
⅓ cup plain yogurt

### DIRECTIONS

In a large bowl, combine apples, celery, raisins, and walnuts. Add mayonnaise and yogurt; toss to coat. Refrigerate, covered, until serving.

*What does cabbage say at the salad bar? Lettuce pray.*

> In 1853, chef George Speck invented potato chips at Moon's Lake House in Saratoga Springs. George, the son of an African American father and Native American mother, later adopted the last name Crum professionally.

# PENNSYLVANIA • PA

## Philly Cheesesteak

**LEVEL 2**

Serves 4

### INGREDIENTS

2 beef ribeye steaks or top round
Salt, to taste
Pepper, to taste
1 tablespoon vegetable oil
1 yellow onion, medium, thinly sliced
4 slices provolone or American cheese or ½ cup Cheez Whiz
4 hoagie rolls

### DIRECTIONS

1. Slice steak as thinly as possible. Season both sides with salt and pepper.
2. Heat oil in a large skillet over medium-high heat. Add sliced onion and sauté until soft, 5 to 7 minutes. Remove and set aside. If not using onion, proceed to next step.
3. Put slices of steak into pan in one layer to sear, 1 to 2 minutes. Flip and sear other side.
4. Use a spatula to chop up steak. Add in cooked onions (if using) and any other desired ingredients.
5. Reduce heat to low and top chopped steak with choice of cheese. Let melt, and then transfer to hoagie rolls. Serve immediately.

**TIP** Have fun by adding other toppings: sautéed bell peppers, sautéed sliced mushrooms, pickled jalapeño slices, sweet peppers, lettuce, tomatoes, mayonaise, and/or mustard.

# PENNSYLVANIA · PA

## Soft Pretzels

**LEVEL 2**

*Makes 12 pretzels*

### INGREDIENTS

1½ cups warm water

2¼ teaspoons instant or active dry yeast

1 teaspoon salt

1 tablespoon unsalted butter, melted and slightly cool

4 cups all-purpose flour, plus more for dusting surface

Coarse sea salt for sprinkling, to taste

**TIP** Watch the video on how to form a pretzel at kitchenink.com. Be creative and make your own pretzel design.

### DIRECTIONS

1. In a large bowl, whisk yeast into warm water. Allow to sit for 1 minute. Whisk in salt and melted butter.

2. Slowly add 3 cups flour, 1 cup at a time. Mix with a wooden spoon until dough is thick. Add ¾ cup more flour until dough is no longer sticky. If it is still sticky, add ¼ to ½ cup more, as needed. Poke dough with your finger—if it bounces back, it is ready to knead.

3. Turn dough out onto a floured flat surface. Knead dough for 3 minutes and shape into a ball. Cover lightly with a towel and allow to rest for 10 minutes.

4. Preheat oven to 400°F. Line 2 baking sheets with parchment paper or silicone baking mats. Silicone baking mats are highly recommended over parchment paper. If using parchment paper, lightly spray with nonstick spray or grease with butter. Set aside.

# PENNSYLVANIA • PA

5. With a sharp knife or pizza cutter, cut dough into 1/3-cup sections.

6. Roll section of dough into a 20- to 22-inch rope. Form a circle with dough by bringing ends together at top of circle. Twist together. Bring twisted ends back down toward yourself and press them down to form a pretzel shape. Repeat with remaining dough.

7. In a large pot, bring ½ cup baking soda and 9 cups water to a boil. Carefully drop 1 or 2 pretzels into boiling water for 20 to 30 seconds. If you leave them in any longer than that, your pretzels will have a metallic taste. Using a slotted spatula, lift pretzel out of water and allow excess water to drip off. Place pretzel onto prepared baking sheet. Sprinkle with coarse sea salt. Repeat with remaining pretzels. If desired, you can cover and refrigerate boiled/unbaked pretzels for up to 24 hours before baking, in step 8.

8. Bake for 12 to 15 minutes or until golden brown.

9. Remove from oven and serve warm.

*Punxsutawney held its first Groundhog Day in Gobbler's Knob on February 2, 1887. According to tradition, if Punxsutawney Phil sees his shadow on February 2, he will be frightened by it and return to his burrow, indicating that there will be six more weeks of winter. If the groundhog does not see his shadow, spring is on the way.*

# RHODE ISLAND • RI

## Frozen Lemonade

**LEVEL 1**

*Makes 1 quart*

### INGREDIENTS

2 lemons
1½ cups water
1½ cups sugar
1½ cups fresh lemon juice
    (approximately 9 medium lemons)
¼ teaspoon kosher salt

**TIP** If you don't have an ice cream machine, use a blender and add 3 cups ice. Blend longer for a smoother frozen drink, and blend less for an icier drink.

### DIRECTIONS

1. Peel skin off lemons with a vegetable peeler. Mince peels to yield 2 tablespoons.
2. In a medium saucepan over medium-high heat, bring 1 cup water, sugar, and lemon peels to a boil until sugar is dissolved and liquid is clear.
3. Remove from heat, stir in ½ cup water, fresh lemon juice, and salt. Remove from stove and chill in the refrigerator approximately 2 hours.
4. Pour chilled liquid into the canister of an ice cream machine to freeze, and process according to the manufacturer's instructions.

NORTHEAST

# RHODE ISLAND · RI

## Johnny Cakes

**LEVEL 2**

*Makes 14 cakes*

### INGREDIENTS

1 cup all-purpose flour
1 cup yellow cornmeal
2½ teaspoons baking powder
1 teaspoon kosher salt
2 large eggs
¾ cup whole milk or buttermilk
¼ cup water
½ cup vegetable oil
2 tablespoons unsalted butter

*Why did the lemon go out with a prune? Because she couldn't find a date.*

### DIRECTIONS

1. In a medium bowl, whisk to combine flour, yellow cornmeal, baking powder, and kosher salt.
2. In a small bowl, beat eggs. Add to flour mixture. Add in milk or buttermilk and water and stir to combine.
3. In a skillet, melt vegetable oil and butter over medium-high heat.
4. Pour ¼ cup batter onto heated pan, flipping once to brown both sides, approximately 5 minutes per side. Remove from heat and repeat with the remaining batter.
5. Serve with butter and maple syrup.

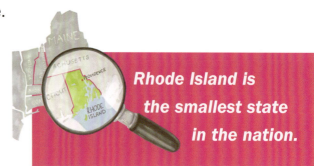

**Rhode Island is the smallest state in the nation.**

# VERMONT • VT

## Maple Candy

**LEVEL 1**

*Makes 12 candies*

### INGREDIENTS

1 cup maple syrup
½ tablespoon butter

### DIRECTIONS

1. Spray candy molds lightly with nonstick spray or coat them with your fingers with a few drops of oil. Wipe away excess with a paper towel.

2. Heat syrup in a large saucepan over medium heat. Once it boils, add butter and stir until melted.

3. Test with a candy thermometer. The temperature should be about 240°F.

4. Remove from heat and allow to cool for a few minutes.

5. Stir vigorously with a wooden spoon until mixture loses its gloss, thickens, lightens in color, and turns opaque.

6. Stop stirring, and don't let mixture cool too much, as it will then be difficult to pour or spoon into molds and may harden in the pan.

7. Work quickly. Pour mixture into molds and smooth with a spatula. As candy cools, it will begin to harden.

8. Let sit at room temperature for about 10 minutes.

9. Pop candies out of molds.

*Did you see the movie about maple syrup? It starts off sappy but ends up sweet.*

# VERMONT · VT

## Macaroni and Cheese

**LEVEL 2**

*Serves 12*

### INGREDIENTS

One 16-ounce package elbow macaroni

6 tablespoons unsalted butter

3 tablespoons all-purpose flour

3 cups whole milk

1½ teaspoons salt

1 teaspoon smoked paprika

½ teaspoon ground black pepper

3½ cups Vermont cheddar cheese, shredded

2 ounces cream cheese

1 cup bread crumbs

### DIRECTIONS

1. Preheat oven to 400°F. Grease a 9 × 13-inch casserole with nonstick spray.
2. Cook macaroni according to directions on package.
3. In a large saucepan, melt 4 tablespoons butter over medium heat. Whisk in flour and cook for 1 minute. Gradually whisk in milk, salt, paprika, and pepper until smooth. Bring to a boil over medium-high heat, whisking constantly, until thickened, about 2 minutes. Lower heat to a simmer. Once simmering, whisk in cheese until smooth.

**TIP** If you are looking to punch up your macaroni and cheese, here are some add-ins you may already have on hand: bacon, broccoli, green beans, peas, carrots, onions, shredded chicken, cracker crumbs.

# VERMONT · VT

4. Add cooked macaroni to cheese sauce. Add cream cheese and stir together until pasta is completely coated and cream cheese is melted. Scoop pasta into casserole.

5. Melt remaining 2 tablespoons butter, mix with bread crumbs, and sprinkle over pasta.

6. Bake for 30 minutes or until lightly browned on top and sides are bubbling.

7. Remove from oven and cool for 5 minutes before serving.

**TIP** Make the Authentic Cincinnati Chili on page 94 and mix some into your macaroni and cheese for a YUMMY chili mac meal.

**Ben & Jerry's headquarters in Waterbury donates ice cream waste to local farmers to feed their hogs—except the mint Oreo flavor, which the hogs don't like!**

# SOUTHEAST

The Southeast is known for the beautiful Great Smoky Mountains, its shoreline of subtropical beaches, its Southern cuisine, and its music, with the country music capital of Nashville. Because of its location and long growing season, the region is rich in natural resources such as rice, cotton, citrus, sugar cane, tobacco, and peanuts. The Southeast also gets oil and natural gas from the Gulf Coast as well as coal and other minerals from the Appalachian Mountains.

## 12 STATES

| | |
|---|---|
| Alabama . . . 36 | Mississippi . . . 52 |
| Arkansas . . . 38 | North Carolina . . . 56 |
| Florida . . . 40 | South Carolina . . . 58 |
| Georgia . . . 42 | Tennessee . . . 60 |
| Kentucky . . . 45 | Virginia . . . 63 |
| Louisiana . . . 48 | West Virginia . . . 66 |

# ALABAMA · AL

## Oven Fried Green Tomatoes

**LEVEL 1**

*Serves 4*

### INGREDIENTS

½ cup buttermilk
1 large egg
⅔ cup fine cornmeal
2 eggs
½ teaspoon salt
1 teaspoon cayenne pepper
2 large green tomatoes, sliced into ¼-inch-thick rounds

### DIRECTIONS

1. Preheat oven to 425°F. Line a large baking sheet with parchment paper.
2. In a shallow bowl, whisk together buttermilk and egg.
3. In a separate bowl, whisk together cornmeal, salt, and cayenne.
4. Dip each tomato slice into buttermilk mixture, letting any excess drip off. Then dip each slice into cornmeal mixture, turning to coat evenly and pressing to adhere. Gently shake each slice to remove any excess.
5. Arrange tomato slices on prepared baking sheet. Coat top of slices with cooking spray and bake for 10 minutes, and then flip slices and coat other side with cooking spray. Bake for 10 minutes more and flip again. Bake for 5 minutes more until lightly browned. Serve piping hot.

**TIP** If you don't have buttermilk on hand, it's easy to make a substitute. For 1 cup buttermilk, pour 1 tablespoon vinegar into a measuring cup, add milk to the 1-cup line, and stir.

# ALABAMA · AL

## Pecan Pie Mini Muffins

**LEVEL 1**

*Makes 12 muffins*

### INGREDIENTS

1 cup brown sugar
½ cup flour
1 cup pecans, chopped
⅔ cup butter, melted
2 eggs

### DIRECTIONS

1. Preheat oven to 350°F and grease a mini muffin pan.
2. In a large bowl, combine sugar, flour, and pecans. Set aside.
3. In a medium bowl, combine melted butter and eggs. Mix well.
4. Stir into flour mixture until combined.
5. Fill each mini muffin cup two-thirds full.
6. Bake for 15 to 20 minutes or until muffins pass the toothpick test: a toothpick inserted in the center comes out clean equals done.
7. Remove and serve immediately.

*The first rocket ship to put humans on the moon was built at NASA's Marshall Space Flight Center in Huntsville, Alabama. The Saturn V rocket launched Apollo 11 on July 16, 1969; four days later the spacecraft successfully landed astronauts Neil Armstrong, Buzz Aldrin, and Michael Collins on the moon.*

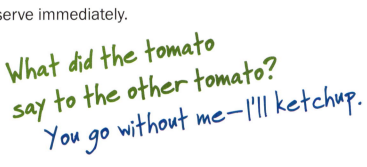

What did the tomato say to the other tomato? You go without me—I'll ketchup.

SOUTHEAST

# ARKANSAS • AR

## Fried Pickles

**LEVEL 2**

*Serves 4*

### INGREDIENTS

½ cup buttermilk

Salt and pepper to taste

One 16-ounce jar dill pickle slices

½ cup all-purpose flour

1½ cups fine cornmeal

1 teaspoon Old Bay® seasoning

¾ teaspoon Cajun seasoning

1 quart oil for frying

One 12-ounce jar ranch dressing

### DIRECTIONS

1. Cover a plate with parchment paper or wax paper.
2. In a shallow dish, combine buttermilk, salt, and pepper. Place pickles in mixture and set aside.
3. Pour flour, cornmeal, Old Bay,® and ¼ teaspoon Cajun seasoning into a large, resealable plastic bag; shake to mix well. Add pickles a few at a time and tumble gently to coat evenly with flour mixture. Remove and place on prepared plate.
4. Have an adult heat oil to 365°F in a deep fryer or a heavy, deep skillet.
5. Fry pickles in several batches until golden brown and slightly crisp on the outside with a moist interior, 1 to 2 minutes. Drain on paper towels. Transfer to serving plate.
6. In a small bowl, combine ranch dressing with ½ teaspoon Cajun seasoning. Serve as a dipping sauce for warm pickles.

# ARKANSAS · AR

## Arkansas Rice Casserole

**LEVEL 1**

Serves 8

### INGREDIENTS

10½ ounces beef broth
1 cup long-grain rice, uncooked
1 cup water
1 onion, diced
1 green pepper, cut into strips
¼ cup butter, melted
4 ounces mushrooms, sliced
2 ounces pimento, drained and diced
1 teaspoon salt

*What happens when life gives you pickles instead of lemons? You dill with it.*

### DIRECTIONS

1. Preheat oven to 375°F. Lightly grease a 12 × 8 × 2-inch baking dish.
2. In a large bowl, combine broth, rice, water, onion, green pepper, butter, mushrooms, pimento, and salt; mix well.
3. Pour mixture into prepared baking dish. Cover with aluminum foil.
4. Bake for 1 hour or until rice is tender. Set timer for 50 minutes and uncover casserole so liquid is absorbed.

**Arkansas's state musical instrument is the fiddle.**

# FLORIDA · FL

## Key Lime Pie

**LEVEL 2**

*Serves 8*

*What did the key lime pie say to the pecan pie? You're nuts.*

### INGREDIENTS

1½ cups graham cracker crumbs
¼ cup sugar
½ teaspoon cinnamon
½ cup butter, melted
One 14-ounce can sweetened condensed milk

3 egg yolks
½ cup fresh squeezed key lime juice
Whipped cream for serving
Lime slices for garnish

### DIRECTIONS

1. Preheat oven to 350°F.
2. In a medium bowl, combine graham cracker crumbs, sugar, and cinnamon and mix together until well combined.
3. Add melted butter and stir until mixture resembles wet sand.
4. Press into a 9-inch pie pan and bake 6–8 minutes.
5. Remove from oven and cool.
6. In a large bowl, combine sweetened condensed milk and egg yolks; whisk until smooth.
7. Add key lime juice and whisk until smooth.
8. Pour filling into pie crust and bake at 350°F for 10 minutes.
9. Cool on a wire rack for 1 hour.
10. Chill pie in the refrigerator 4 hours or overnight.
11. Top with whipped cream and garnish with lime slices.

# FLORIDA · FL

## Sunburst Drink

**LEVEL 1**

*Serves 4*

### INGREDIENTS

6 ounces orange frozen concentrate (½ can)

1 cup milk

¼ cup sugar

1 teaspoon vanilla extract

2 cups ice cubes

Orange slices for garnish

### DIRECTIONS

1. Put orange juice concentrate, milk, sugar, vanilla extract, and ice cubes into blender.
2. Blend until smooth.
3. Pour into glasses and hang an orange slice on rim of each glass.

*Orange juice is Florida's official state drink (adopted in 1967).*

SOUTHEAST

# GEORGIA • GA

## No-Bake Peanut Butter Pie

**LEVEL 1**

Serves 8

*What did the guest say when it went to the peanut butter's dinner party? Nice spread.*

### INGREDIENTS

**CRUST**

2 cups Oreo cookie crumbs

5 tablespoons butter, melted

**FILLING**

Two 8-ounce packages cream cheese, softened

1 cup confectioners' sugar

1 teaspoon vanilla extract

¾ cup creamy peanut butter

1 cup heavy whipping cream, whipped into stiff peaks

8 peanut butter cups for garnish

### DIRECTIONS

1. Lightly grease a 9-inch pie plate.
2. In a medium bowl, combine Oreo cookie crumbs and melted butter. Press crumbs into bottom of pie plate and put in freezer for 10 minutes.
3. In a large bowl, mix together cream cheese, confectioners' sugar, and vanilla extract until creamy and smooth. Add peanut butter and mix well. Fold in whipped cream until well blended.
4. Spread filling into Oreo crust and smooth out top. Cover with plastic wrap and refrigerate until set, approximately 3 to 4 hours, or overnight.
5. Remove from refrigerator and top with more whipped cream. Garnish with peanut butter cups if you choose.

# GEORGIA • GA

## Southern Fried Chicken

**LEVEL 3**

*Serves 4*

### INGREDIENTS

1½ cups milk
2 large eggs
2½ cups all-purpose flour
2 tablespoons salt,
    plus additional for sprinkling
2 teaspoons black pepper
4 pounds bone-in, skin-on chicken pieces
Vegetable oil for frying

**TIP** For moister Southern Fried Chicken, replace milk with buttermilk. Soak chicken pieces in a buttermilk marinade for at least 6 hours. This marinading ensures the chicken comes out juicy and can help the flour stick better.

### DIRECTIONS

1. Preheat oven to 200°F and place a rack in a large baking pan.
2. In a medium bowl, combine milk and eggs. Whisk to blend well.
3. In a large, heavy-duty resealable plastic food storage bag, combine flour, salt, and pepper. Seal and shake to combine.
4. Dip chicken pieces in milk and egg mixture and let excess drip off into bowl. Set already dipped pieces aside on a plate until you have three or four.
5. Add dipped chicken pieces to bag of seasoned flour.
6. Seal bag and shake well to coat chicken pieces thoroughly.
7. Remove to a plate and repeat with remaining chicken pieces.
8. Heat oil in a deep, heavy skillet to 350°F. While it's heating up, line a large serving plate with paper towels and set aside.

# GEORGIA • GA

9. Fry chicken a few pieces at a time for about 10 minutes on each side, or until golden brown and thoroughly cooked. Be careful not to put too many pieces in at once—even if they comfortably fit—since doing so will dramatically drop the oil's temperature, affecting the crispness of the final product. Note that chicken breasts will take a little less time to fry than dark meat pieces.

10. With a slotted spoon, move done chicken pieces onto paper towel-lined platter to drain. Sprinkle immediately with salt.

11. Transfer drained and seasoned chicken to prepared pan with a rack. Keep warm in preheated oven while frying subsequent batches. Depending on the size of your pan, this recipe will require about 3 to 4 batches.

Georgia grows the most peanuts in the United States.

# KENTUCKY • KY

## Hot Brown Sandwiches

**LEVEL 2**

Serves 4

### INGREDIENTS

#### CHEESE SAUCE

4 tablespoons butter

¼ cup all-purpose flour

2 cups whole milk

2 cups sharp cheddar cheese, shredded

½ teaspoon Worcestershire sauce

Salt and pepper, to taste

#### SANDWICHES

4 slices bread, toasted

8 slices cooked turkey breast

4 slices baked ham

8 slices fresh, ripe tomato

8 slices bacon, cooked

### DIRECTIONS

#### CHEESE SAUCE

1. In a medium saucepan, melt butter over low heat. Whisk in flour and cook, whisking for 3 minutes.
2. Whisk in milk, raise heat to medium, and continue cooking, stirring, until very thick.
3. Stir in cheese and continue cooking, stirring, until cheese melts.
4. Stir in Worcestershire sauce and season to taste with salt and pepper.
5. Set aside and keep warm.

# KENTUCKY • KY

**SANDWICHES**

1. Preheat oven to 400°F. Line a rimmed baking sheet with parchment paper.
2. Place toast slices in one layer on prepared baking sheet.
3. Put 2 slices of turkey and 1 of ham on each piece of toast.
4. Place 2 slices of tomato on top of each sandwich, overlapping if needed.
5. Spoon cheese sauce over top.
6. Top each sandwich with 2 slices of bacon, making an X shape.
7. Bake until sauce bubbles, around 8 to 10 minutes. Serve immediately.

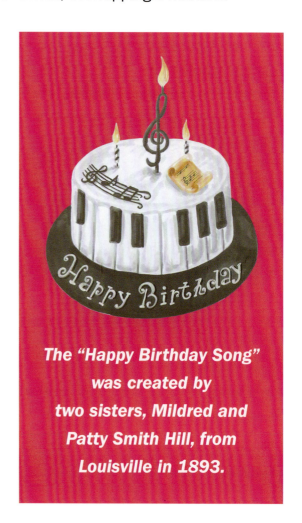

The "Happy Birthday Song" was created by two sisters, Mildred and Patty Smith Hill, from Louisville in 1893.

46  RECIPE ROAD TRIP

# KENTUCKY • KY

## Kentucky Derby Pie

**LEVEL 2**

*Serves 10*

### INGREDIENTS

One 9-inch, deep-dish pie crust, unbaked

4 large eggs

¾ cup brown sugar

¾ cup light corn syrup

½ cup flour

½ cup butter, melted and cooled

¼ cup sugar

1½ teaspoons vanilla extract

1¼ cups pecans, chopped

¾ cup miniature semisweet chocolate chips

*What do Kentucky Derby horses eat? Fast food.*

### DIRECTIONS

1. Preheat oven to 350°F.
2. In a medium bowl, whisk together eggs, brown sugar, corn syrup, flour, butter, white sugar, and vanilla extract.
3. Fold pecan pieces and chocolate chips into egg mixture until combined; pour into prepared pie crust.
4. Bake until pie is set, 45 to 50 minutes. Serve warm or chilled.

# LOUISIANA • LA

## Easy King Cake

**LEVEL 1**

*Serves 8*

### INGREDIENTS

2 cans store-bought cinnamon rolls
¼ cup sugar
1 drop each yellow, green, red, and blue food coloring
1 porcelain or plastic toy baby (optional)

### DIRECTIONS

1. Preheat oven to 375°F. Grease a large cookie sheet or line it with a silicone baking mat.

2. Arrange cinnamon rolls sideways in a circular pattern on cookie sheet. Press down on rolls with your hand to flatten slightly; flattened rolls will look like a cake. If including, add toy baby in middle of dough.

3. Bake according to package instructions.

4. Make colored sugar. Divide sugar into three small bowls. Put 1 drop yellow food coloring into one; using your fingers, grind color into sugar until all granules are colored. Do the same using green food coloring. In third cup, blend 1 drop red food coloring and 1 drop blue food coloring to make purple, and then color sugar in same way.

5. Allow cake to cool for a few minutes on a wire rack. Drizzle with icing included in rolls' package. Sprinkle colored sugar randomly over icing. Slice across width of cake into eight thick slices to serve.

**TIP** This cake traditionally contains a tiny porcelain or plastic baby that is supposed to bring good luck to whoever winds up with it in their slice.

48  RECIPE ROAD TRIP

# LOUISIANA · LA

## Yeti Baked Alaska

**LEVEL 3**

*Serves 8 to 10*

### INGREDIENTS

1 pint vanilla ice cream
12 ounces blueberries, frozen
One 15.25-ounce box yellow cake mix
2 tablespoons blue candy sprinkles

#### MERINGUE

1 cup sugar
⅓ cup water
4 egg whites
1 pinch cream of tartar

### DIRECTIONS

Steps 1 and 2 need to happen a minimum of 1 hour or up to 24 hours before preparing cake.

1. Make purple ice cream: process vanilla ice cream and blueberries in a food processor until well blended.

2. Line a 2-quart bowl with plastic wrap, leaving edges long to fully cover ice cream. Scoop ice cream into bowl and place bowl in freezer.

3. Preheat oven to 350°F. Grease and line with parchment paper a 17-inch jelly roll pan (rimmed cookie sheet).

"Baked Alaska" was supposedly coined in 1867 at Antoine's, a New Orleans restaurant, by its chef de cuisine, Antoine Alciatore, to honor the United States' acquisition of Alaska from the Russian Empire on March 10, 1867.

# LOUISIANA • LA

4. Make cake mix according to package instructions, adding blue sprinkles to raw batter. Pour batter into prepared pan and bake for 25 minutes or until cake springs back to touch. Let cake cool for 15 to 20 minutes.

5. Take bowl of ice cream from freezer and remove ice cream from bowl.

6. Cut cake in half vertically and place ice cream dome on top of half of the cake. Press remaining cake on and around the dome and sides until the cake covers all the ice cream.

7. Using fondant (see recipe, facing page), make a half-circle face for the Yeti out of blue fondant. For the eyes, use a water bottle top to cut two circles out of white fondant. For the teeth, cut six triangles out of white fondant. For the mouth, roll out black fondant and cut out a smile wide enough to contain the teeth, and affix triangle teeth as you like. For the eyeballs, cut out two black circles and place on top of larger white circles. Place Yeti in freezer while you prepare meringue.

8. In a small pan fitted with a sugar thermometer, stir sugar and water until dissolved. Heat gently until mixture starts to thicken and turn yellow (240°F).

9. Whisk egg whites and cream of tartar to soft peaks and slowly drizzle in the hot syrup, whisking constantly until mixture is stiff and glossy. Spoon into a piping bag fitted with a large round nozzle.

10. Remove Yeti from freezer and, starting around the arch of the face, hold the piping bag at a 90-degree angle and gently squeeze. Once a small amount of meringue has touched the cake, stop squeezing and lift the piping bag, forming a peak or a long spike. Continue to cover all sides of the cake except the face to form the Yeti's fur. Return Yeti to freezer until ready to serve.

# LOUISIANA · LA

## Fondant

**LEVEL 1**

You can purchase white, black, and blue fondant icing, or make your own with this easy recipe.

### INGREDIENTS

Cornstarch
2 cups marshmallow creme
4 cups confectioners' sugar
Food coloring, black and blue

### DIRECTIONS

1. Dust a 9 × 13-inch sheet of parchment paper with cornstarch and set aside.
2. In a bowl, mix marshmallow creme and sugar and form a ball.
3. Place ball on prepared parchment paper and place in the microwave.
4. Microwave on high for 20 seconds; fondant should be smooth. If not, microwave for a few additional seconds.
5. Depending on number of colors, divide ball into sections and knead a different color into each section.
6. Sprinkle flat surface with cornstarch and, using a rolling pin, roll fondant to desired thickness.

*Why did the boy eat his homework?*
*His friend said it was a piece of cake.*

# MISSISSIPPI • MS

## Mississippi Mud Pie

**LEVEL 3**

*Serves 8*

### INGREDIENTS

#### OREO CRUST

20 Oreo cookies

⅓ cup salted butter, melted

#### FUDGE BROWNIE LAYER

½ fudge brownie mix, plus ingredients to prepare mix according to package

#### WHIPPED CREAM

3 cups heavy whipping cream

½ cup sugar

1½ teaspoons vanilla extract

¼ teaspoon cream of tartar

#### CHOCOLATE PUDDING LAYER

One 3.9-ounce box instant chocolate pudding

2 tablespoons cocoa powder

2 cups whole milk

1 teaspoon vanilla extract

#### TOPPINGS

Crushed Oreos

Chocolate shavings

Hot fudge

# MISSISSIPPI • MS

### DIRECTIONS

#### OREO CRUST

1. Preheat oven to 350°F. Grease a 9-inch pie pan.
2. In a food processor or blender, pulse Oreo cookies until finely ground. Add melted butter and pulse until everything is saturated and well combined.
3. Evenly press mixture into base and onto sides of pie pan. Bake for 10 to 15 minutes, or until firm.

#### FUDGE BROWNIE LAYER

1. In a medium-sized bowl, prepare brownie mix according to package directions and combine until smooth. Use only half of mix.
2. Pour brownie batter into prebaked crust. Use a spatula to evenly spread batter. Bake for 15 to 20 minutes, or until a toothpick stuck in the middle comes out clean.
3. Set pie pan on a cooling rack and let it cool completely, about 2 hours. Brownies should be room temperature before adding pudding layer.

#### WHIPPED CREAM

1. In a large bowl, using a mixer, beat heavy whipping cream on medium speed until it begins to thicken.
2. Add sugar, vanilla extract, and cream of tartar. Turn mixer onto high speed and continue to beat until soft peaks form.
3. Cover and refrigerate until ready to use.

#### PUDDING LAYER

1. In a large bowl, whisk together pudding mix and cocoa. Add in milk and vanilla extract, and then whisk for 2 minutes. Let stand for 5 minutes to thicken.

# MISSISSIPPI • MS

2. Gently fold in 2 cups of whipped cream you refrigerated earlier. Mix only until just combined.
3. Refrigerate pudding until ready to use.

### ASSEMBLY

1. Remove pie crust and whipped cream from refrigerator.
2. Spoon pudding into pie pan on top of brownie layer and let cool for 20 minutes.
3. Spoon whipped cream on top of pudding layer and top with chocolate shavings and/or crushed Oreos.

*The state is named after the Mississippi River, which the Ojibwa called messipi—"Big River."*

# MISSISSIPPI • MS

## Pimento Cheese

**LEVEL 1**

*Serves 4*

### INGREDIENTS

8 ounces cream cheese, softened

2 cups cheddar cheese, shredded

1 cup packed, coarsely grated Monterey Jack cheese

⅓ cup light mayonnaise

2 tablespoons pimentos, chopped

½ teaspoon onion powder

Ground black pepper, to taste

Celery sticks or crackers for serving

### DIRECTIONS

1. In a medium bowl, beat cream cheese until fluffy.

2. Beat in cheddar cheese, Monterey Jack cheese, mayonnaise, pimentos, onion powder, and pepper until well blended.

3. Serve with celery sticks, crackers, or other vegetables of your choice.

*I bought a pack of animal-shaped biscuits but had to take it back, as the seal was broken.*

# NORTH CAROLINA • NC

## Sweet Potato Balls

**LEVEL 2**

Serves 4

### INGREDIENTS

4 large sweet potatoes
⅔ cup brown sugar, packed
2 tablespoons orange juice
1 teaspoon orange zest
¼ teaspoon freshly grated nutmeg
½ cup granulated sugar
1 teaspoon ground cinnamon
1 large marshmallow per potato ball

*Why can't you get angry at a yam? Because they are such sweet potatoes.*

### DIRECTIONS

1. Preheat oven to 350°F. Grease a baking sheet.
2. Bake potatoes until tender, and then peel and mash them.
3. In a medium bowl, combine mashed potatoes, brown sugar, orange juice, zest, and nutmeg.
4. In a separate bowl, stir together sugar and cinnamon.
5. Press mashed potatoes around each marshmallow, creating a 2- to 3-inch-diameter ball.
6. Roll each ball in sugar mixture.
7. Place balls two inches apart on baking sheet and bake for 15 to 20 minutes.

**TIP** Don't overbake this dish, as marshmallows may expand and burst the potato balls.

# NORTH CAROLINA • NC

## Creamy Coleslaw

**LEVEL 1**

*Serves 6*

### INGREDIENTS

1 small head green cabbage, quartered, cored, and thinly sliced or shredded

2 large carrots, shredded

1 cup mayonnaise

1½ tablespoons sugar

1 teaspoon celery seed

3 tablespoons white vinegar

1 teaspoon lemon juice

Salt and pepper, to taste

### DIRECTIONS

1. In a large bowl, toss cabbage and carrots to combine.
2. In a medium bowl, prepare dressing: whisk and combine mayonnaise, sugar, celery seed, vinegar, lemon juice, salt, and pepper.
3. Pour dressing over cabbage mixture and stir to coat evenly. Cover and refrigerate 1 hour prior to serving.

*Putt-putt golf was created in 1954 in Fayetteville by Don Clayton and became a global phenomenon.*

# SOUTH CAROLINA • SC

## Shrimp and Grits

**LEVEL 2**

Serves 4

*What do shrimp wear in the kitchen?*
*A-Prawns.*

### INGREDIENTS

4 cups water
½ teaspoon salt
½ teaspoon pepper
1 cup stone-ground grits
3 tablespoons butter
2 cups sharp cheddar cheese, shredded

1 pound shrimp, peeled and deveined
6 slices bacon, chopped
4 teaspoons lemon juice
2 tablespoons parsley, chopped
1 cup scallions, thinly sliced
1 large garlic clove, minced

### DIRECTIONS

1. In a large pot, bring water to a boil. Add salt, pepper, and grits and cook until water is absorbed, about 20 to 25 minutes.
2. Remove from heat and stir in butter and cheese.
3. Rinse shrimp and pat dry.
4. In a large skillet, fry bacon until browned. Drain well, reserving grease, and transfer to a plate.
5. In the same skillet, add shrimp and reserved grease and cook until shrimp turn pink. Add lemon juice, bacon, parsley, scallions, and garlic. Sauté for 3 minutes.
6. Spoon grits into a serving bowl, add shrimp mixture, and mix well. Serve immediately.

# Frogmore Stew

**LEVEL 2**

Serves 4 to 6

> No people live on 4,500-acre Morgan Island. The only inhabitants are a colony of 3,500 free-ranging, Indian-origin rhesus macaque monkeys.

### INGREDIENTS

- 1½ gallons water
- 1 lemon, juiced
- ½ teaspoon salt
- 3 tablespoons Old Bay® seasoning
- 16 red skin new potatoes
- 2 pounds andouille sausage or your choice kielbasa, cut into ½-inch slices
- 10–12 ears of corn, shucked and cut into 3-inch pieces
- 4 pounds jumbo shrimp, uncooked in shell
- Butter, room temperature, for corn
- Cocktail sauce, for shrimp

### DIRECTIONS

1. In a large stock pot over medium-high heat, add water, lemon, salt, and Old Bay® seasoning and bring to a boil.
2. Add potatoes to pot and boil for an additional 20 minutes. When done, potatoes should easily be pierced by a knife.
3. Add sausage to pot and boil uncovered for 5 minutes.
4. Add corn and cook for 5 minutes; water does not need to come to a boil.
5. Add shrimp to pot and cook an additional 3 to 5 minutes.
6. Remove pot from the heat and drain.
7. Traditionally, a tabletop is covered with paper, and the stew is dumped on the table for people to scoop into their bowls—no silverware needed.

**NOTE** This stew contains no frogs. It originated in Frogmore, a small Lowcountry fishing community on St. Helena Island near Beaufort and Hilton Head. The dish is also sometimes called Lowcountry boil or Beaufort stew.

SOUTHEAST

# TENNESSEE • TN

## Nashville Hot Chicken

**LEVEL 3**

*Makes 4 large servings*

### INGREDIENTS

#### DRY BRINE

1 whole chicken, cut into quarters
1 tablespoon kosher salt
1½ teaspoons black pepper, freshly ground

#### DIP

1 cup whole milk
2 large eggs
1 tablespoon Louisiana-style hot sauce

#### DREDGE

2 cups all-purpose flour
2 teaspoons sea salt
Vegetable oil for frying

#### SPICY COATING

3 tablespoons cayenne pepper (reduce to make milder)
1 tablespoon light brown sugar, packed
1 teaspoon black pepper, freshly ground
¾ teaspoon sea salt
½ teaspoon paprika
½ teaspoon garlic powder

#### FOR SERVING

White bread
Dill pickle slices for garnish

### DIRECTIONS

1. In a medium bowl, toss together chicken pieces, salt, and pepper. Cover and refrigerate overnight (up to 24 hours).
2. In a shallow bowl, whisk together milk, eggs, and hot sauce (for milder chicken, reduce hot sauce).
3. In a second shallow bowl, combine flour and salt.

60  RECIPE ROAD TRIP

# TENNESSEE • TN

4. Drag chicken piece through flour mixture, coating evenly.

5. Dip floured chicken in milk mixture.

6. Shake off excess and drag chicken a second time in flour mixture.

**TIP** The spice level in this recipe is gauged as medium-hot. Adjust spices according to your taste.

7. Allow chicken to rest on a drying rack while you prepare rest of chicken pieces for frying.

8. In a deep skillet or deep fryer, heat vegetable oil until it is between 340° and 350°F. Oil needs to be deep enough to fully submerge chicken.

9. Working in batches, use tongs to carefully add chicken to hot oil and fry until crispy. Turn pieces as they brown. Do not let them touch each other while frying.

10. Estimated cooking times are 15 to 17 minutes for breast quarters and 18 to 20 minutes for leg quarters. Chicken is done when its internal temperature registers 165°F. When done, remove chicken from oil and allow to drain on wire rack.

11. In a small saucepan, add 1 cup oil and whisk in cayenne pepper, brown sugar, pepper, salt, paprika, and garlic powder. Heat over medium heat and use to baste fried chicken, only enough to keep skin crispy.

12. In Nashville, a hot piece of chicken is served on a slice of white bread garnished with dill pickle slices.

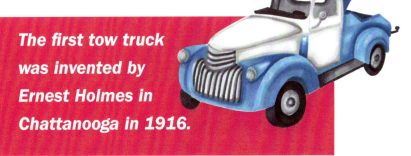

*The first tow truck was invented by Ernest Holmes in Chattanooga in 1916.*

SOUTHEAST

# TENNESSEE • TN

## Banana Pudding

**LEVEL 2**

*Serves 10*

*If you had five oranges in one hand and five pears in the other hand, what would you have? Massive hands.*

### INGREDIENTS

- 2 cups milk
- 1 teaspoon vanilla extract
- Two 3.4–ounce instant vanilla pudding packages
- 14 ounces sweetened condensed milk
- 2 cups heavy whipping cream
- 3 tablespoons confectioners' sugar
- 11 ounces vanilla wafers
- 4 bananas, sliced

### DIRECTIONS

1. In a large bowl, beat milk with vanilla extract and vanilla pudding until it thickens. Pour in condensed milk and beat to combine.

2. In a separate bowl, beat heavy whipping cream until smooth peaks form. Add about two-thirds of whipped cream to pudding and gently fold in with a spatula.

3. Add confectioners' sugar into remaining third whipped cream and fold with a spatula to combine. Refrigerate until needed.

4. Layer about one-fourth of vanilla wafers into bottom of a trifle bowl and about one-fourth of bananas. Spread one-fourth of pudding over bananas/wafers. Repeat layering until you have four layers.

5. Top with reserved whipped cream and decorate top as you wish. Cover and refrigerate 2 hours prior to serving.

**TIP** If you don't have a classic trifle bowl or big glass vase on hand, use a glass mixing bowl so you can see all the dish's pretty layers.

# VIRGINIA • VA

## Boiled Peanuts

**LEVEL 1**

*Serves 12*

### INGREDIENTS

2 pounds raw peanuts

¼ cup salt

### DIRECTIONS

1. Place peanuts in a sink of water and gently scrub to remove dust and dirt.
2. Place in a colander, rinse again, and let drain.
3. Fill a large pot three-quarters full with water and add peanuts.
4. Over medium-high heat, bring to a boil.
5. Cover pot, reduce heat to medium, and let boil for 3 hours.
6. Add salt and more water if needed. Continue cooking.
7. An adult should carefully spoon out peanuts to taste every 30 minutes until cooked to desired doneness.
8. Remove from heat and let cool.
9. Serve warm.

# VIRGINIA • VA

## Ham and Cheese Biscuits

**LEVEL 3**

*Serves 10*

### INGREDIENTS

2½ cups all-purpose flour

1 tablespoon plus 1 teaspoon baking powder

One 4-ounce stick salted butter, cold

4 ounces sharp cheddar cheese, grated

½ cup cooked ham, diced

1 cup buttermilk

2 tablespoons butter, melted

1 teaspoon parsley, chopped

### DIRECTIONS

1. Preheat oven to 475°F. Line baking sheet with parchment paper and set aside.

2. In a large bowl, add flour and baking powder. Grate cold butter and add to flour mixture. Toss together to combine. Place in freezer for 10 minutes.

3. Remove from freezer and toss in cheddar cheese and ham until evenly combined with flour mixture. Create a well at bottom of bowl and pour in buttermilk. Mix with a wooden spoon about 15 times around. It's okay if it's not completely mixed.

4. Flour a flat kneading surface (a counter is fine). Pour biscuit mixture onto prepared surface and work with your hands until mixture is no longer dry and crumbly. Flour a rolling pin and roll out the dough into a rectangle until it's about ¾ inch thick. Fold in half so the short edges touch. Rotate dough and repeat this four more times, adding flour as needed to prevent sticking. Roll out into final rectangle that is about ¾ inch thick.

# VIRGINIA • VA

*What do you call a pig that gets fired from his job? Canned ham!*

5. Using a biscuit cutter, cut out biscuits and place on prepared baking sheet so that biscuits are touching. Combine remaining scraps and roll out again and cut more biscuits until all the dough is used.

6. Bake biscuits for 13 to 15 minutes, or until they start to brown at the edges. Remove from oven.

7. Add chopped parsley to melted butter and stir together. Brush butter mixture over tops of biscuits while they're still hot. Let them cool for a few minutes and serve warm.

*The first known recipe for ketchup comes from an 1824 Virginia cookbook.*

# WEST VIRGINIA • WV

## Pepperoni Rolls

**LEVEL 3**

*Makes 8 rolls*

### INGREDIENTS

1½ cups milk
3 tablespoons unsalted butter
2 tablespoons sugar
2 teaspoons kosher salt
2 teaspoons active dry yeast
3½ cups all-purpose flour, plus more for dusting

1 large egg
One 6-ounce pepperoni stick, cut into 4 logs and each cut in half lengthwise
¼ cup extra virgin olive oil
1½ cups mozzarella, shredded

### DIRECTIONS

1. Line 2 baking sheets with parchment paper and set aside.
2. In a small saucepan, gently heat milk and butter until butter is melted. Temperature should be between 100° and 115°F. Remove from heat and whisk in sugar, salt, and yeast. Let mixture sit until yeast is activated and foam covers the top, 5 to 8 minutes.
3. Add flour to a large bowl and make a well in the center. Crack the egg into the middle and pour in yeast liquid. Mix all ingredients together with a silicone spatula. Make sure all ingredients are incorporated and form a sticky, loose dough. Cover bowl with plastic wrap and let rise in a warm place for 2 hours. The dough will double in size.
4. Remove plastic wrap and gently re-knead dough while it is still in the bowl.
5. Form into a ball, cover in plastic wrap, and rest in a warm place for 1 hour.

# WEST VIRGINIA • WV

6. After an hour, remove dough to a flat, floured surface, kneading to bring together. Cut dough into 8 pieces. Gently form each piece of dough into balls, using more flour as needed.

7. Use your hands to flatten each ball into a 4½-inch circle.

8. Brush a piece of pepperoni with oil and place in the center of one circle along with 2 tablespoons shredded mozzarella. Fold dough over pepperoni like a wrap, and place on baking sheet seam side down.

9. Repeat with remaining pepperoni logs. Allow 1 inch space between rolls on baking sheets. Cover both baking sheets with plastic wrap and leave in a warm place for a half hour prior to baking. The rolls will continue to rise.

10. While rolls continue to rise, preheat oven to 350°F.

11. Brush tops of rolls with remaining oil and bake for 30 to 35 minutes. Rolls will have a golden color and crispy edges.

**Mother's Day was first observed as a holiday at Andrews Church in Grafton on May 10, 1908. It became a national holiday in 1914.**

# WEST VIRGINIA • WV

## Skillet Cornbread

**LEVEL 2**

*Serves 8 to 10*

### INGREDIENTS

1¼ cups coarsely ground cornmeal
¾ cup all-purpose flour
¼ cup sugar
1 teaspoon kosher salt
2 teaspoons baking powder

2 teaspoons baking soda
⅓ cup whole milk
1 cup buttermilk
2 eggs, lightly beaten
8 tablespoons unsalted butter, melted

### DIRECTIONS

1. Preheat oven to 425°F and place a 9-inch cast-iron skillet inside to heat while you make batter.

2. In a large bowl, whisk together cornmeal, flour, sugar, salt, baking powder, and baking soda. Whisk in milk, buttermilk, and eggs. Whisk in almost all the melted butter, reserving about 1 tablespoon for the skillet later on.

3. Using a pot holder, carefully remove hot skillet from oven. Reduce oven temperature to 375°F.

4. Coat bottom and sides of skillet with remaining butter. Pour batter into skillet and place it in center of oven.

5. Bake 20 to 25 minutes or until center is firm and a toothpick inserted into center comes out clean. Allow to cool for 10 to 15 minutes and serve with Honey Butter (recipe on facing page).

*What do you tell cornbread after it graduates from college? Corn-gratulations.*

# WEST VIRGINIA • WV

## Honey Butter

**LEVEL 1**

Salted or unsalted butter can be used. If you use salted, do not add kosher salt. Make sure your butter is softened to room temperature, not cold and hard as a rock, and not melted. Room-temperature butter whips up nice and creamy!

### INGREDIENTS

½ cup unsalted butter, room temperature
3 tablespoons honey
½ teaspoon kosher salt

### DIRECTIONS

1. Place butter in a mixing bowl; beat with an electric mixer until light and fluffy. Add in honey and salt; beat until combined and smooth.

2. Scrape down sides of bowl with a spatula and beat again until perfectly light and fluffy.

3. Spoon into a ramekin or a 4-ounce glass jar. Leave on the counter, covered, for up to two days, or transfer to the refrigerator in an airtight container for longer storage, up to two weeks (bring to room temperature before serving). You can even freeze it up to two months. Thaw overnight in the refrigerator and bring to room temperature before serving.

## MIDWEST

What some call "America's Heartland," the Midwest is known for its industry, farming, and residents with friendly, down-to-earth attitudes. Rich soil and plentiful water help make the Midwest one of the country's major farming regions. Many important crops and production come from the Midwest, including corn, wheat, dairy, livestock, and iron ore.

**12 STATES**

- Illinois . . . 72
- Indiana . . . 75
- Iowa . . . 79
- Kansas . . . 81
- Michigan . . . 83
- Minnesota . . . 85
- Missouri . . . 87
- Nebraska . . . 89
- North Dakota . . . 91
- Ohio . . . 93
- South Dakota . . . 96
- Wisconsin . . . 98

# ILLINOIS · IL

## Chicago-Style Pizza

**LEVEL 2**

*Makes 2 pizzas*

### INGREDIENTS

#### DOUGH

3½ cups all-purpose flour
¼ cup cornmeal
¼ ounce quick-rise yeast
1½ teaspoons sugar
½ teaspoon salt
1 cup water
⅓ cup olive oil

#### TOPPINGS

6 cups part-skim mozzarella cheese, shredded
One 28-ounce can diced tomatoes, drained
8 ounces tomato sauce
6 ounces tomato paste
½ teaspoon salt
¼ teaspoon garlic powder
¼ teaspoon dried oregano
¼ teaspoon dried basil
¼ teaspoon black pepper
1 pound Italian sausage, cooked and crumbled
48 slices pepperoni
½ pound fresh mushrooms, sliced
¼ cup Parmesan cheese, grated

### DIRECTIONS

1. In a large bowl, combine 1½ cups flour, cornmeal, yeast, sugar, and salt.
2. In a saucepan, heat water and oil to 130°F. Add to dry ingredients; beat just until moistened. Add remaining flour to form a stiff dough.
3. Flour a flat surface and knead dough until smooth and elastic, approximately 6 to 8 minutes.

*What is a dog's favorite type of pizza?*
*Pupperoni.*

# ILLINOIS • IL

4. Grease a medium-sized bowl; turn dough to grease all sides. Cover bowl with plastic wrap and let dough rise in a warm place until doubled in size, approximately 30 minutes.

5. Punch dough down and divide in half. Roll each portion into an 11-inch circle.

6. Grease the bottom of two 10-inch cast-iron skillets. Place one dough circle in each skillet and sprinkle with 2 cups mozzarella cheese.

**TIP** If you don't own a cast-iron skillet, any oven-proof skillet will work.

7. In a large bowl, combine tomatoes, tomato sauce, tomato paste, and seasonings.

8. Spoon 1½ cups sauce over each pizza. Then layer each with half of sausage, pepperoni, and mushrooms, 1 cup mozzarella, and 2 tablespoons Parmesan cheese.

9. Cover and bake at 450°F for 35 minutes. Uncover; bake until lightly browned, about 5 additional minutes.

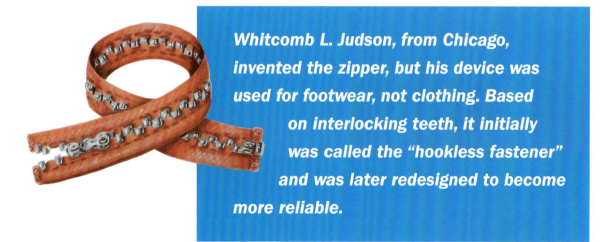

*Whitcomb L. Judson, from Chicago, invented the zipper, but his device was used for footwear, not clothing. Based on interlocking teeth, it initially was called the "hookless fastener" and was later redesigned to become more reliable.*

MIDWEST 73

# ILLINOIS · IL

## Chicago-Style Hot Dog

**LEVEL 1**

Serves 1

### INGREDIENTS

1 all-beef hot dog
1 poppy seed hot dog bun
1 tablespoon yellow mustard
1 tablespoon sweet green pickle relish
1 tablespoon onion, chopped
4 tomato wedges
2 sport peppers
1 dash celery salt
1 dill pickle spear

**TIP** Sport peppers are small, hot, pickled peppers; substitute green peppers if you don't want heat.

### DIRECTIONS

1. In a small pot, bring water to a boil. Reduce heat to low, add hot dog, and cook approximately 5 minutes. Remove from water and set aside.
2. Put a steamer on top of the pot and steam hot dog bun for no more than 2 minutes.
3. Place hot dog in bun and layer toppings in the following order: yellow mustard, pickle relish, onion, tomato wedges, sport peppers, celery salt.
4. Place pickle spear between hot dog and bottom of the bun.

# INDIANA • IN

## Classic Pork Tenderloin Sandwiches

**LEVEL 3**

*Serves 4*

### INGREDIENTS

One 12-ounce pork tenderloin, sliced into four 1-inch fillets, butterflied

1 cup flour

2 eggs

3 tablespoons whole milk

40 saltine crackers (1 sleeve)

1 tablespoon onion powder

1 teaspoon garlic powder

1 teaspoon salt

1 cup vegetable oil, enough to fill a large skillet ½ inch deep

4 hamburger buns

### TOPPINGS

Lettuce leaves

Red onion, sliced

Pickles, sliced

Yellow mustard

### DIRECTIONS

1. Line a baking sheet with paper towels and place a cooling rack on top; set aside.
2. Trim and pound pork to ¼-inch to ⅜-inch thickness.
3. Put flour in a bowl.
4. In a shallow bowl, beat eggs and milk together.
5. In a food processor, chop saltines; add onion powder, garlic powder, and salt and pulse to combine. Pour into a shallow bowl.
6. Dip pork fillet in flour, then in egg mixture, and then in saltine crumbs. Press on crumbs.
7. In a cast-iron skillet, heat vegetable oil to 350–375°F.

# INDIANA · IN

8. Place fillet in oil for 1½ to 2 minutes, until crumbs are browned. Flip fillet to brown other side.
9. Remove from oil and place on cooling rack; set baking sheet to warm in oven.
10. Repeat process until all fillets are cooked.
11. Lightly butter and toast buns.
12. Serve each fillet on a hamburger bun with lettuce, pickles, onion, and mustard.

Indiana has a town named Popcorn.

76  RECIPE ROAD TRIP

# INDIANA · IN

## Sugar Cream Pie

**LEVEL 3**

*Serves 8*

### INGREDIENTS

1 single, prebaked pie crust

#### PIE FILLING

4½ tablespoons cornstarch
1 cup granulated sugar
1 pinch of salt
3 cups heavy cream
5 tablespoons unsalted butter, cut into cubes
1 tablespoon vanilla extract

#### TOPPING

2 tablespoons unsalted butter, melted
1 teaspoon ground cinnamon
¼ teaspoon ground nutmeg

### DIRECTIONS

1. Bake a frozen or refrigerated crust.
2. Once crust is cooled, cover outer edges with strips of aluminum foil to prevent burning while topping is broiled. Place crust on a rimmed baking sheet and set aside.
3. In a medium saucepan, whisk together cornstarch, sugar, and a pinch of salt. Add cream and butter. Cook over medium heat, whisking constantly to prevent scorching until mixture thickens and begins to boil. Cook 1 minute more, and then remove from the heat.
4. Add vanilla extract and whisk to combine.
5. Pour filling into prebaked pie crust. Gently jiggle pan to distribute filling evenly in pie plate.

# INDIANA • IN

6. While pie rests, with a pot holder and adult assistance, move oven rack up to about 6 inches from heating element. Preheat oven to broil with the door propped open.

7. After pie filling sets for 15 to 30 minutes, drizzle melted butter over top of pie. Tilt pie to distribute butter evenly.

8. Combine cinnamon and nutmeg and sift over pie filling.

9. Place pie under the broiler and cook until butter bubbles and the surface browns. This takes less than a minute, so keep your eye on it.

10. Cool pie completely and then refrigerate for at least 4 hours or overnight, or until center is set.

*What is a ghost's favorite dessert?*
*Boo-berry pie.*

# IOWA • IA

## Sweet and Easy Corn on the Cob

**LEVEL 1**

*Serves 6*

### INGREDIENTS

2 tablespoons sugar

1 tablespoon lemon juice

6 ears of corn on the cob, husks and silks removed

### DIRECTIONS

1. Fill a large pot about three-quarters full of water and bring to a boil.
2. Stir in sugar and lemon juice, dissolving sugar.
3. Gently place ears of corn into boiling water, cover the pot, turn off the heat, and let corn cook in hot water until tender, about 10 minutes.
4. Using tongs, carefully remove ears of corn from the pot.

*What do you call the state fair in Iowa? A corn-ival.*

MIDWEST 79

# IOWA • IA

## Egg and Sweet Corn Frittata

**LEVEL 2**

*Serves 3*

### INGREDIENTS

1 cup sweet corn
1 cup tomatoes,
    seeds removed, chopped
1⅓ cups zucchini, chopped
⅔ cup red onion, chopped
6 eggs, beaten
¼ teaspoon salt
¼ teaspoon pepper
⅛ cup bacon, crumbled (optional)

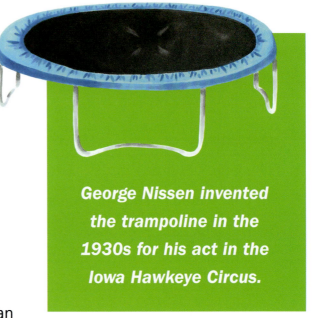

*George Nissen invented the trampoline in the 1930s for his act in the Iowa Hawkeye Circus.*

### DIRECTIONS

1. Preheat oven to 400°F. Grease a pie pan and set aside.
2. In a large bowl, combine corn, tomatoes, zucchini, and red onion. Add in eggs, salt, and pepper and stir.
3. Pour into pie pan and place in oven. Bake 20 to 25 minutes. Top of pie will be golden and firm.
4. Remove from oven and sprinkle with bacon (if using). Serve immediately.

# KANSAS · KS

## Brown Sugar Oat Muffins

**LEVEL 2**

*Makes 12 muffins*

### INGREDIENTS

1 cup old-fashioned oats
1 cup whole wheat flour
¾ cup brown sugar, packed
½ cup all-purpose flour
2 teaspoons baking powder
½ teaspoon salt
2 large eggs, room temperature
¾ cup milk
¼ cup canola oil
1 teaspoon vanilla extract

### DIRECTIONS

1. Preheat oven to 400°F. Grease or paper-line cups of a muffin tin.
2. In a medium bowl, combine oats, whole wheat flour, sugar, all-purpose flour, baking powder, and salt.
3. In another medium bowl, whisk together eggs, milk, oil, and vanilla extract. Add to oat mixture; stir just until moistened.
4. Fill muffin cups two-thirds full. Bake 15 to 17 minutes or until a toothpick inserted in center comes out clean.
5. Cool 5 minutes before removing muffins to a wire rack. Serve warm.

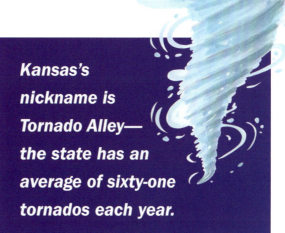

*Kansas's nickname is Tornado Alley— the state has an average of sixty-one tornados each year.*

MIDWEST 81

# KANSAS · KS

*Why couldn't the teddy bear finish his muffin? Because he was stuffed.*

## Wholesome Wheat Bread

**LEVEL 2**

*Makes 2 loaves*

### INGREDIENTS

2 packages (¼ ounce each) active dry yeast

2¼ cups warm water

⅓ cup butter, softened

⅓ cup honey

3 tablespoons sugar

1 tablespoon salt

½ cup nonfat milk

4½ cups whole wheat flour

3½ cups all-purpose flour

### DIRECTIONS

1. In a large bowl, dissolve yeast in warm water. Add butter, honey, sugar, salt, milk, and 3 cups whole wheat flour. Beat on medium speed until smooth. Stir in remaining flour to form a soft dough.

2. Flour a flat surface and knead dough until smooth and elastic, approximately 10 minutes.

3. Place dough in a greased bowl, turning to grease top of dough; cover bowl and let dough rise in a warm place until doubled in size, approximately 1 hour.

4. Punch down dough. Turn onto a lightly floured surface, and divide dough into four portions.

5. Roll each portion into a 15-inch rope. For each loaf, twist two ropes together; pinch ends to seal.

6. Place in two greased 9 × 5-inch loaf pans. Cover with kitchen towels; let rise in a warm place until doubled, about 30 minutes.

7. Preheat oven to 375°F. Bake until golden brown, 25 to 30 minutes.

8. Remove from pans to wire rack to cool.

# MICHIGAN • MI

## Cherry Salad

**LEVEL 1**

*Serves 8*

### INGREDIENTS

7 ounces fresh baby spinach
3 ounces spring mix greens
1 large apple, chopped
½ cup toasted pecans, chopped
½ cup cherries, dried
¼ cup Gorgonzola cheese, crumbled

### DRESSING

¼ cup fresh raspberries
¼ cup red wine vinegar
3 tablespoons apple cider vinegar
3 tablespoons cherry preserves
1 tablespoon sugar
2 tablespoons olive oil

The first soda pop made in the United States was Vernor's Ginger Ale, created in Detroit in 1866.

### DIRECTIONS

1. In a large bowl, combine spinach, greens, apple, pecans, cherries, and cheese.
2. Place raspberries, vinegars, preserves, and sugar in a blender. While processing, gradually add oil in a steady stream.
3. Drizzle over salad; toss to coat.

*Why did the cherry go to the chocolate factory?*
*It was cordially invited.*

MIDWEST 83

# MICHIGAN • MI

## Cherry Pie

**LEVEL 2**

*Serves 8*

### INGREDIENTS

1 cup plus 1 tablespoon sugar
3 tablespoons cornstarch
¼ teaspoon salt
⅔ cup cherry juice
Two 2½-pound bags frozen sour cherries

½ teaspoon almond extract
2 tablespoons butter
Pastry for double-crust 9-inch pie
2 teaspoons milk

### DIRECTIONS

1. Preheat oven to 400°F.
2. In a large saucepan, combine I cup sugar, cornstarch, and salt, stirring to remove lumps. Stir cherry juice into sugar mixture. Cook over medium heat until smooth, stirring constantly. Add cherries. Simmer until liquid is thickened and transparent, about 4 minutes. Stir once or twice. Add almond extract and butter, stirring until butter melts. Allow mixture to cool.
3. On a lightly floured sheet of waxed paper, roll half of pastry to ⅛-inch thickness. Place in a 9-inch deep-dish pie plate; trim off excess pastry along edges. Pour cooled cherry mixture into pastry shell.
4. Roll remaining pastry to ⅛-inch thickness; cut into strips, if you want to make a lattice-topped pie. Otherwise, transfer entire pastry to top of pie. Trim off excess pastry along edges and cut slits in top crust for steam to escape.
5. Brush top of pastry shell lightly with milk or cream, and sprinkle pastry with 1 tablespoon sugar.
6. Bake for 55 minutes or until golden brown.

# MINNESOTA • MN

## Minnesota Hot Dish Casserole

**LEVEL 1**

*Serves 8*

### INGREDIENTS

1 pound ground beef
¼ cup onion, chopped
¼ teaspoon salt
10.75 ounces cream of mushroom soup
½ cup milk
16 ounces frozen mixed vegetables
1 cup cheddar cheese, shredded
32 ounces tater tots

*In 1919, a Minnesota mechanic named Charles Strite created an easy-to-use toaster designed for restaurants. In 1921, he received his patent for the automatic pop-up toaster.*

### DIRECTIONS

1. Preheat oven to 400°F and use a nonstick spray to oil a 2½-quart baking dish.
2. In a skillet over medium heat, brown ground beef, onion, and salt. Drain and spoon into baking dish.
3. In a small bowl, combine soup and milk and mix well.
4. Layer frozen vegetables over ground beef. Top with soup mixture and cheese.
5. Top with tater tots and bake for approximately 30 minutes or until tots are golden brown.

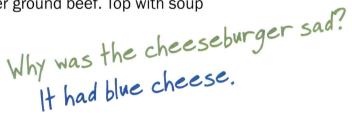

*Why was the cheeseburger sad? It had blue cheese.*

# MINNESOTA • MN

## Blueberry Muffins

**LEVEL 1**

*Makes 12 muffins*

### INGREDIENTS

½ cup butter, softened

1¼ cups plus 3 teaspoons sugar

2 eggs

2 cups flour

½ teaspoon salt

2 teaspoons baking powder

½ cup milk

2 cups fresh blueberries

1 teaspoon freshly grated orange peel

### DIRECTIONS

1. Preheat oven to 375°F. Grease or put paper liners in large muffin cups.
2. In a medium bowl, cream butter and 1¼ cups sugar until light and fluffy. Add eggs one at a time, beating well after each.
3. Sift together flour, salt, and baking powder.
4. Add dry mixture to creamed mixture, alternately with milk.
5. Crush ½ cup blueberries with a fork and mix into batter. Fold in remaining whole berries and add orange peel.
6. Fill muffin cups three-quarters full and sprinkle tops with remaining 3 teaspoons sugar.
7. Bake for 20 to 30 minutes. Cool for 30 minutes before removing from muffin tin.

# MISSOURI • MO

## Fried Ravioli

**LEVEL 2**

Serves 4

### INGREDIENTS

1 egg
2 tablespoons milk
½ teaspoon kosher salt
½ teaspoon black pepper
¾ cup Italian seasoned bread crumbs
10 ounces ravioli, any flavor, fresh or frozen
¼ cup extra virgin olive oil
Marinara sauce, for serving
Parmesan cheese, for garnish
Fresh parsley, chopped, for garnish

*Why didn't the ravioli get invited to hang out with the cool pastas?*

*Because he was a little square.*

### DIRECTIONS

1. In a shallow bowl, mix egg, milk, salt, and pepper.
2. Place bread crumbs in another shallow bowl.
3. With one hand, dip each ravioli into egg and milk mixture, shaking gently to remove excess. Place in the bread crumbs and bread each side thoroughly, using your other clean hand to pat bread crumbs into the surface. Place breaded ravioli on a baking sheet or large plate.
4. Heat olive oil in a large, heavy skillet over medium-high heat. When oil is hot, carefully add ravioli to skillet. Fry for about 2 minutes on each side, until breadcrumb coating is golden brown. Remove to a paper towel–lined plate or baking sheet.
5. Allow time to cool. Serve with marinara sauce and garnish with Parmesan cheese and parsley.

# MISSOURI • MO

## Ozark Sloppy Joes

**LEVEL 2**

*Serves 8*

### INGREDIENTS

1½ pounds ground beef
1 medium green pepper, chopped
1 small onion, chopped
2 teaspoons sugar
1½ teaspoons all-purpose flour
1½ teaspoons Italian seasoning
½ teaspoon chili powder
¼ teaspoon salt
¼ teaspoon garlic powder
⅛ teaspoon cayenne pepper
8 ounces tomato sauce
1½ teaspoons Worcestershire sauce
8 hamburger buns, split

### DIRECTIONS

1. In a large skillet over medium heat, cook beef, green pepper, and onion until meat is no longer pink. Drain.

2. Stir in sugar, flour, seasonings, tomato sauce, and Worcestershire sauce. Cover and simmer for 10 to 15 minutes, stirring occasionally.

3. Spoon one-half cup of sloppy joe on each bun.

*In 1908, at the St. Louis Fair, Abe Doumar created the first waffle cone.*

# NEBRASKA • NE

## Classic Reuben Sandwiches

**LEVEL 2**

*Makes 3 sandwiches*

### INGREDIENTS

**RUSSIAN DRESSING**

¼ cup mayonnaise
1½ teaspoons chili garlic sauce
½ teaspoon lemon juice
1½ teaspoons creamy horseradish
1 garlic clove, minced
½ teaspoon Worcestershire sauce
½ tablespoon onion, finely grated
⅛ teaspoon paprika
Salt and pepper, to taste

**SANDWICHES**

½ teaspoon olive oil
½ pound corned beef
6 slices rye bread
2 tablespoons unsalted butter, room temperature
½ cup sauerkraut, drained
6 slices Swiss cheese

### DIRECTIONS

1. In a medium bowl, combine all ingredients for Russian dressing: mayonnaise, chili garlic sauce, lemon juice, horseradish, garlic, Worcestershire sauce, onion, paprika, salt, and pepper. Set aside.

2. In a skillet, over medium heat, add oil. Once hot, add meat and cook just until heated.

3. Lightly butter one side of each slice of bread. Place bread butter side down on a plate. Add toppings to each sandwich: spread dressing, and top with meat, 2 slices cheese, and sauerkraut. Place a piece of bread on top.

4. In a hot skillet, cook sandwiches over medium heat 4 to 6 minutes, flipping once. Cook until cheese melts and bread is crispy.

# NEBRASKA • NE

## Corn Fritters

**LEVEL 2**

*Makes 12 to 14 fritters*

### INGREDIENTS

2 eggs, beaten
½ teaspoon salt
½ teaspoon pepper
2 teaspoons sugar
1 teaspoon baking powder
3 tablespoons flour
1½ cups whole corn, drained
2 tablespoons butter

*Why shouldn't you tell a secret on a farm? Because the potatoes have eyes and the corn have ears.*

### DIRECTIONS

1. In a large bowl, mix together eggs, salt, pepper, sugar, baking powder, flour, and corn.

2. In a skillet, heat butter and drop 2 tablespoons of batter to form a small oval cake.

3. Cook over medium heat about 5 minutes or until brown on both sides. Turn only once. Repeat until you have used all the batter.

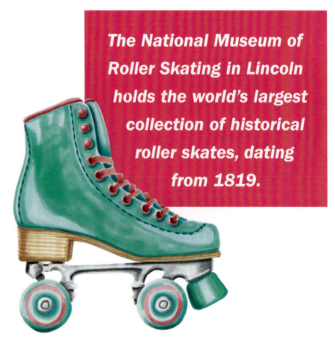

The National Museum of Roller Skating in Lincoln holds the world's largest collection of historical roller skates, dating from 1819.

90  RECIPE ROAD TRIP

# NORTH DAKOTA • ND

## Chippers
## (Chocolate-Covered Potato Chips)

**LEVEL 1**

*Makes 24 chips*

### INGREDIENTS

12 ounces semisweet chocolate chips

5 cups ridged potato chips

### DIRECTIONS

1. Microwave chocolate in 30-second increments and stir between each time until fully melted.

2. Dip each chip almost all the way in, and then tap gently to remove excess chocolate.

3. Allow to cool and dry on a baking sheet lined with parchment paper.

# NORTH DAKOTA • ND

## Honey Vanilla French Toast

**LEVEL 2**

*Serves 4*

### INGREDIENTS

3 eggs
¾ cup milk
¼ cup heavy whipping cream
1 tablespoon honey
1 tablespoon vanilla extract
1 tablespoon ground cinnamon
2 tablespoons unsalted butter
8 slices sourdough bread

North Dakota is the number-one producer of honey and sunflowers in the United States.

### DIRECTIONS

1. In a small bowl, beat eggs together with milk and cream.
2. Add honey, vanilla extract, and cinnamon and whisk thoroughly.
3. Heat a large skillet and melt 1 tablespoon butter.
4. Soak each piece of bread in egg mixture for 5 to 10 seconds.
5. Add bread to skillet, leaving space between pieces. Cook on both sides for 2 to 3 minutes until golden brown.
6. Serve warm with butter, maple syrup or jam, and fresh berries.

*Why do bees have sticky hair? Because they use honey combs!*

# OHIO • OH

## Buckeyes

**LEVEL 2**

*Makes 30 pieces*

### INGREDIENTS

1 cup smooth peanut butter

4 tablespoons unsalted butter, softened

1 teaspoon vanilla extract

¼ teaspoon salt

2 cups powdered sugar

8 ounces semisweet chocolate chips

### DIRECTIONS

1. In a large bowl with an electric mixer, stir peanut butter, butter, vanilla extract, and salt on medium speed until ingredients combine. Add powdered sugar using low speed and increasing to medium as mixture combines.

2. Line a cookie sheet with wax paper and roll out peanut butter mixture into 1-inch balls. Once baking sheet is full, freeze the balls for 30 minutes to harden.

3. Melt chocolate. Using toothpicks as skewers, dip chilled peanut butter balls in chocolate. Cover all but the top of each ball.

4. Place dipped buckeyes back onto the baking sheet and smooth over the hole left by the toothpick.

5. Refrigerate buckeyes until chocolate sets. Store leftover buckeyes in an airtight container in the refrigerator.

# OHIO • OH

## Authentic Cincinnati Chili

**LEVEL 2**

*Makes 10 large servings*

### INGREDIENTS

2 pounds lean ground beef
1 quart water, or amount to cover beef
2 onions, finely chopped, with additional for topping
One 15-ounce can tomato sauce
2 tablespoons vinegar
4 garlic cloves, minced
2 teaspoons Worcestershire sauce
1 ounce unsweetened chocolate
1½ tablespoons chili powder
1½ teaspoons salt
1 teaspoon ground cumin
1 teaspoon ground cinnamon
½ teaspoon ground cayenne pepper (optional)
5 whole cloves
¾ teaspoon allspice
1 teaspoon freshly ground black pepper
1 bay leaf
Cooked spaghetti for serving

*Unlike all the other state flags, Ohio's flag is not rectangular. Its pennant design is one-of-a-kind. According to the Ohio State Flag Code, the flag is to be folded seventeen times, to represent Ohio as the seventeenth state to join the union.*

# OHIO • OH

**DIRECTIONS**

1. Place ground beef in a large pot, cover with cold water, and bring to a boil, stirring and breaking up beef to a fine texture with a fork. Slowly boil until meat is thoroughly cooked, about 30 minutes.

2. Add onions, tomato sauce, vinegar, garlic, Worcestershire sauce, and chocolate. Stir in chili powder, salt, cumin, cinnamon, and cayenne pepper (if using) until well mixed. Add cloves, allspice, pepper, and bay leaf.

3. Bring to a boil, reduce heat to a simmer, and cook, stirring occasionally, for 3 hours. Add water if necessary to prevent chili from burning.

4. Serve in bowls with toppings of your choice.

**Toppings:** Build your bowl with spaghetti, chili, and cheese, and then top it off with onions, kidney beans, or even oyster crackers.

*When did the peanut butter say it would arrive?*
*In a Jiffy.*

# SOUTH DAKOTA • SD

## Kuchen

**LEVEL 2**

*Serves 8 to 10*

### INGREDIENTS

**CAKE**

½ cup butter, melted
½ cup sugar
1 large egg
½ tablespoon almond extract
1 cup sour cream
1½ cups all-purpose flour
¾ teaspoon baking powder

**TOPPING**

¼ cup butter, softened
¼ cup sugar
¼ cup brown sugar
¼ cup all-purpose flour
⅛ teaspoon cloves, crushed
¼ teaspoon cinnamon
3 cups peaches, peeled and sliced thin

### DIRECTIONS

1. Preheat oven to 350°F. Grease a 9 × 13-inch pan.
2. In a large bowl, cream together butter and sugar. Blend in egg, almond extract, and sour cream. Mix in flour and baking powder. Spread dough in prepared pan.
3. In a small bowl, mix butter, sugar, brown sugar, flour, cloves, and cinnamon to create the topping.
4. Sprinkle half of topping over cake dough, place peach slices over entire surface, and sprinkle remaining topping to cover the kuchen.
5. Bake on center rack of oven for 30 to 35 minutes. Check cake at 30 minutes and if it comes out with crumbs on it, it's done.
6. Kuchen can be served hot out of the oven, but cooling it for 2 to 3 hours is recommended, as the clove flavor becomes milder and all flavors soften.

**TIP** You may substitute plums, pears, or blueberries for peaches.

RECIPE ROAD TRIP

# SOUTH DAKOTA · SD

## Oven-Roasted Vegetables

**LEVEL 2**

*Serves 12*

### INGREDIENTS

1 pound Yukon Gold potatoes
1 pound Brussels sprouts
1 medium onion
½ pound broccoli florets
3 large carrots
½ pound cauliflower florets
1 large sweet potato
3 garlic cloves, minced
¼ cup olive oil
¼ teaspoon kosher salt
¼ teaspoon black pepper

*Mitchell, South Dakota, is the home of the world's only Corn Palace, built with 3,500 bushels of ear corn. Murals in the palace are made from corn and other grains and grasses such as wild oats, rye, straw, and wheat. Each year entirely new murals are created.*

### DIRECTIONS

1. Preheat oven to 375°F. Place a large, rimmed baking sheet on center rack to heat up along with the oven.

2. Rinse and cut vegetables into uniform pieces, each about 1 square inch. Place all vegetables and garlic in a large bowl and drizzle with olive oil. Toss to coat and season with salt and pepper.

3. Once oven is preheated, (carefully!) pour prepared vegetables onto the hot pan and spread into an even layer. Bake for 75 to 90 minutes, tossing 35 minutes into cooking so that vegetables evenly brown. Remove from oven when vegetables are browned and crispy, and serve immediately.

*How do you know if an egg joke is good? If it cracks you up.*

# WISCONSIN • WI

## Cheese Fondue

**LEVEL 1**

*Serves 8*

### INGREDIENTS

⅓ pound firm alpine-style cheese, such as Gruyère, grated
⅓ pound fontina, grated
⅓ pound Gouda, grated
2 tablespoons cornstarch

1 cup vegetable broth
1 clove garlic, minced
1 tablespoon fresh lemon juice
1 teaspoon Dijon mustard
⅛ teaspoon nutmeg

### DIRECTIONS

1. In a medium bowl, grate all cheeses. Add in cornstarch and toss to coat.

2. In a stove-safe fondue pot or large, heavy saucepan, bring broth, garlic, and lemon juice to a simmer over medium-low heat. Add cheeses to simmering liquid a little at a time, stirring well between each addition to ensure a smooth fondue. Once smooth, stir in mustard and nutmeg.

3. Arrange an assortment of bite-size dipping foods on a platter. If necessary, carefully pour fondue into a fondue pot. Serve with fondue forks or wooden skewers. Dip and enjoy!

**TIP** Be sure to use high-quality cheeses for this dish.

**Dipping suggestions:** Apples—tart Granny Smiths (cut into cubes) taste best. Bread—cut a sourdough baguette into 1-inch cubes for easy skewering. Cherry tomatoes, oven-crisp bacon, roasted baby potatoes, potato chips, steamed broccoli, and pickles are other options. Experiment with your favorite foods.

# WISCONSIN • WI

## Wisconsin Cheese Soup

**LEVEL 2**

*Makes 4 (1-cup) servings*

### INGREDIENTS

3½ cups chicken broth
½ cup chopped carrot
1 small onion, chopped
1 rib celery, chopped
½ cup milk
20 ounces American cheese, roughly chopped
4 drops hot pepper sauce (or less if you don't want heat)
⅓ cup all-purpose flour

*Wisconsin's state dance is the polka. A World of Accordions, a museum with more than 1,000 types of squeeze-boxes, is found in the state.*

### DIRECTIONS

1. In a 4-quart saucepan, add 1 cup chicken broth, carrot, onion, and celery.
2. Cook over medium-high heat 8 to 10 minutes or until onion is softened.
3. Add 2 cups chicken broth, milk, cheese, and hot pepper sauce (if using). Reduce heat to medium; cook 5 to 8 minutes or until cheese is melted.
4. In a medium bowl, add flour and stir in remaining chicken broth until smooth. Stir flour mixture into soup. Cook, stirring constantly, 1 to 2 minutes or until soup is slightly thickened.

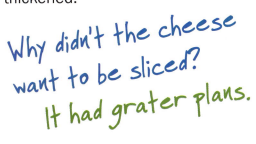

*Why didn't the cheese want to be sliced? It had grater plans.*

MIDWEST 99

# SOUTHWEST

The southwestern United States is known for its arid deserts, red rock landscapes, rugged mountains, and natural wonders like the Grand Canyon. Uranium, coal, and natural gas are all found in the Southwest, though the region's most important natural resource is oil.

## 4 STATES

**Arizona . . . 102**

**New Mexico . . . 105**

**Oklahoma . . . 108**

**Texas . . . 110**

# ARIZONA • AZ

## Baked Chicken Chimichangas

**LEVEL 3**

Serves 4

### INGREDIENTS

2 cups cooked chicken, shredded
1 tablespoon chili powder
½ teaspoon cumin
¼ teaspoon paprika
½ teaspoon salt
½ cup salsa
2 cups Colby-Jack cheese, shredded
2 ounces cream cheese, softened
2 tablespoons green onions, chopped
One 15-ounce can refried beans
Four 10-inch tortillas
1 tablespoon olive oil

*Why can't you trust a burrito? They tend to spill their beans.*

### DIRECTIONS

1. Preheat oven to 400°F.
2. In a medium-sized mixing bowl, combine chicken, chili powder, cumin, paprika, salt, salsa, Colby-Jack cheese, cream cheese, and green onions.
3. For each tortilla, spoon 2 tablespoons refried beans onto tortilla 2 inches from the edge. Put about ½ cup of meat mixture into the center. Fold in sides of tortilla, roll up the bottom, and place seam side down on a baking sheet. Brush tops with olive oil. Bake for 20 minutes or until golden brown and heated through.
4. Serve warm.

# ARIZONA · AZ

## Breakfast Burritos with Avocado-Tomato Salsa

**LEVEL 3**
*Serves 4*

### INGREDIENTS

**AVOCADO-TOMATO SALSA**

1 large avocado, peeled, pitted, and diced
½ cup tomatoes, seeded and diced
1 small shallot, minced
1 clove garlic, minced
1 jalapeño pepper, seeded and minced
1 tablespoon fresh lime juice
½ teaspoon salt
¼ teaspoon ground cumin
¼ cup fresh cilantro, chopped

**BURRITOS**

4 large eggs
¼ teaspoon smoked paprika
¼ teaspoon salt
½ pound spicy sausage (chorizo or Italian), removed from casings
1⅓ cups Monterey Jack cheese, shredded
Four 10-inch flour tortillas
Vegetable oil

### DIRECTIONS

1. In a medium bowl, add avocado, tomatoes, shallot, garlic, jalapeño pepper, lime juice, salt, cumin, and cilantro. Set aside.

2. In a medium bowl, whisk eggs with smoked paprika and salt. Set aside.

3. In a large nonstick pan over medium-high heat, add sausage and cook, stirring frequently, until browned, 4 to 5 minutes. With a slotted spoon, transfer sausage from pan to a plate, leaving drippings in the pan.

4. Reduce heat to low. Add eggs and scramble until just cooked through. Transfer eggs to a plate.

# ARIZONA • AZ

**ASSEMBLY**

1. Spoon about ¼ cup of salsa onto each tortilla, followed by a quarter of the sausage, a quarter of the eggs, and ⅓ cup cheese.
2. Lightly coat pan with oil and set over medium heat. When pan is hot, add burritos, seam side down. Cook, covered, until bottom of burritos is golden brown, about 3 minutes. Flip burritos over and continue cooking, covered, until golden.
3. Serve warm.

*Yuma is the sunniest city in the world, as it is sunny 90 percent of the time. Its proximity to the equator—around 2,300 miles away—means it gets a lot of the sun's energy.*

# NEW MEXICO • NM

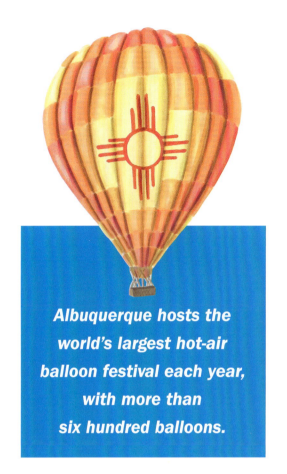

Albuquerque hosts the world's largest hot-air balloon festival each year, with more than six hundred balloons.

## Guacamole

**LEVEL 1**

*Makes 2 cups*

### INGREDIENTS

2 ripe avocados
½ teaspoon salt
1 garlic clove, finely minced
1 teaspoon fresh lime juice or to taste
1 medium-sized tomato, chopped
¼ cup red onion, finely chopped
1 medium-size jalapeño, minced
2 tablespoons fresh cilantro, coarsely chopped

### DIRECTIONS

1. Halve and pit the avocados and scoop pulp into a medium bowl.
2. Add salt and garlic; add lime juice to taste.
3. Fold in tomato, onion, chile and cilantro. Let stand a few minutes before serving to allow flavors to blend. Taste and adjust seasonings as necessary.

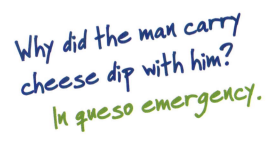

Why did the man carry cheese dip with him?
In queso emergency.

SOUTHWEST 105

# NEW MEXICO • NM

## Huevos Rancheros

**LEVEL 3**

*Serves 4*

### INGREDIENTS

#### SALSA

1 tablespoon extra virgin olive oil

½ medium onion, chopped

15 ounces crushed tomatoes

6 ounces diced green chiles

½ teaspoon chipotle chili powder, adobo sauce, regular chili powder, or ground cumin, or to taste (optional)

Salt, to taste

#### HUEVOS RANCHEROS

4 corn tortillas

1 teaspoon olive oil

2 teaspoons butter

4 large eggs

2 tablespoons fresh cilantro, chopped (optional)

2 ripe avocados, peeled, pitted, and sliced, for garnish

### DIRECTIONS

#### SALSA

1. In a large skillet over medium heat, sauté onions in olive oil. Once onions are translucent, add tomatoes and their juice.

2. Add chopped green chiles. Add chipotle chili powder or other seasoning.

3. Bring to a simmer, reduce heat to low, and let simmer while you do the rest of the cooking, stirring occasionally. Add salt, to taste.

106 RECIPE ROAD TRIP

# NEW MEXICO · NM

### HUEVOS RANCHEROS

1. Preheat oven to 150°F. Place serving plates in oven to keep warm.

2. Over medium-high heat, coat a large nonstick skillet with 1 teaspoon olive oil.

3. One by one (or more, if your pan is big enough) heat tortillas in the pan, 1 or 2 minutes on each side, until they are heated through, softened, and pockets of air bubble up inside them.

4. Remove and stack tortillas on one of the plates in the oven to keep warm while you continue cooking the rest of tortillas and eggs.

5. Using the same skillet you used for the tortillas, add a little butter to the pan, about 2 teaspoons for 4 eggs. Heat pan to medium-high. Crack eggs into skillet and cook 3 to 4 minutes for runny yolks, a minute or two longer for firmer eggs.

6. To serve, spoon a little sauce onto a warmed plate. Top with a tortilla, then a fried egg. Top with more sauce, sprinkle with cilantro if desired, and garnish with avocado slices.

# OKLAHOMA • OK

## Chicken-Fried Steak

**LEVEL 3**

Serves 4

### INGREDIENTS

2½ cups all-purpose flour
2 tablespoons salt
1 teaspoon cayenne pepper (optional)
3 eggs, beaten
3 pounds beef chuck steaks

1 cup oil for frying
2½ cups milk
1 teaspoon garlic salt
¾ teaspoon celery salt
1 cup beef broth

### DIRECTIONS

1. In a shallow bowl, combine 2 cups flour, salt, and cayenne pepper (if using); set aside.

2. In another shallow bowl, beat together eggs and remaining ½ cup flour.

3. Pound steaks flat with a meat mallet. Coat steaks first in flour mixture, then in egg mixture, and again in flour.

4. In a large skillet, over medium-high heat, heat the oil and cook coated steaks until golden brown. Remove from skillet, drain all but 1 tablespoon oil, and keep steaks warm.

5. To make gravy, add seasoned flour to remaining oil in skillet and cook over medium heat, stirring constantly, until flour is browned. Remove from heat and stir in milk, garlic salt, celery salt, and beef broth. Return to the heat and bring to a simmer, stirring constantly, until gravy thickens.

6. Serve chicken fried steak with gravy and mashed potatoes and your favorite green veggies.

*Why was the little strawberry crying? His parents were in a jam.*

# OKLAHOMA · OK

## Oklahoma Cheese Grits

**LEVEL 2**

*Serves 4*

### INGREDIENTS

6 cups water
1½ cups quick-cooking grits
¾ cup butter
1 pound Velveeta cheese, cubed
2 teaspoons seasoning salt
1 tablespoon Worcestershire sauce
½ teaspoon hot pepper sauce (optional)
2 teaspoons salt
3 eggs, beaten

*Sylvan Goldman, owner of the Humpty Dumpty grocery store chain, invented the shopping cart in 1936 in Oklahoma City.*

### DIRECTIONS

1. Preheat oven to 350°F. Lightly grease a 9 × 13-inch baking dish.
2. In a medium-sized saucepan, bring water to a boil. Stir in grits and reduce heat to low. Cover, and cook 5 to 6 minutes, stirring occasionally.
3. Mix in butter, cheese, seasoning salt, Worcestershire sauce, hot pepper sauce (if using), and salt. Continue cooking for 5 minutes, or until cheese is melted.
4. Remove from heat, cool slightly, and fold in eggs. Pour into prepared baking dish.
5. Bake 1 hour, or until top is lightly browned.

**TIP** Mix up the cheese—use American, cheddar, Colby, or Monterey Jack.

SOUTHWEST

# TEXAS • TX

## Slow Cooker Texas Pulled Pork

**LEVEL 1**

*Makes 8 sandwiches*

### INGREDIENTS

1 teaspoon vegetable oil
One 4-pound pork shoulder roast
1 cup barbecue sauce
¼ cup apple cider vinegar
½ cup chicken broth
¼ cup light brown sugar
1 tablespoon yellow mustard

1 tablespoon Worcestershire sauce
1 tablespoon chili powder
1 extra-large onion, chopped
2 large garlic cloves, crushed
1½ teaspoons dried thyme
8 hamburger buns, split
2 tablespoons butter

### DIRECTIONS

1. Pour vegetable oil into the bottom of a slow cooker. Place pork roast in the slow cooker; pour in barbecue sauce, vinegar, and chicken broth. Stir in brown sugar, yellow mustard, Worcestershire sauce, chili powder, onion, garlic, and thyme. Cover and cook on low for 10 to 12 hours or high for 5 to 6 hours until pork shreds easily with a fork.

2. Remove pork from the slow cooker and shred meat using two forks. Return shredded pork to the slow cooker and stir to combine with juices.

3. Spread the inside of both halves of hamburger buns with butter. Toast buns, butter side down, in a skillet over medium heat until golden brown. Spoon pulled pork into toasted buns.

*Why did the skeleton go to the barbecue?*
*He needed some spare ribs!*

# TEXAS · TX

## Country Potato Salad

**LEVEL 1**

*Serves 6*

### INGREDIENTS

6–8 medium Yukon Gold potatoes, peeled (about 2 pounds)
¼ cup red onion, chopped finely
3 stalks celery, chopped finely
3 eggs, hard boiled, chopped

#### DRESSING

1 cup mayonnaise
2 teaspoons yellow mustard
¼ cup sweet relish
1 teaspoon salt
½ teaspoon black pepper
½ teaspoon paprika, plus more for garnish if desired

*Bracken Cave, on the northern outskirts of San Antonio, is home to the world's largest bat colony, with more than 15 million Mexican free-tailed bats. During summer evenings the bats take flight into the Texas sky, forming a massive, swirling cloud that may be the largest single gathering of mammals on Earth.*

### DIRECTIONS

1. Add potatoes to a large pot, cover with water (1 to 2 inches above potatoes), and cook until fork-tender.
2. Remove potatoes from pot, let cool for 10 minutes, and cut into 2-inch cubes.
3. In a large bowl, add chopped potatoes, onion, celery, and eggs.
4. In a small bowl, combine mayonnaise, mustard, relish, salt, pepper, and paprika and whisk until well combined.
5. Add dressing to potatoes and stir gently to combine.
6. Cover and store in refrigerator until ready to serve.

# WEST

This land is filled with great mountains, volcanoes, rolling plains, fertile valleys, beaches, and deserts. The region's natural resources include trees, salt, and oil. The Rocky Mountains also are rich in minerals such as copper, gold, and silver. Much of the wood used in the United States comes from the West; wood products include lumber, plywood, cardboard, and paper. Pineapples and potatoes are two of the region's many crops.

## 11 STATES

Alaska . . . 114
California . . . 117
Colorado . . . 120
Hawaii . . . 122
Idaho . . . 124
Montana . . . 127
Nevada . . . 132
Oregon . . . 134
Utah . . . 136
Washington . . . 138
Wyoming . . . 140

# ALASKA · AK

## Salmon Croquettes

**LEVEL 2**

*Serves 20*

### INGREDIENTS

2 cups mashed potatoes
Two 6.5-ounce cans cooked salmon
2 scallions, finely chopped
2 teaspoons fresh lemon juice
1 tablespoon fresh parsley, chopped
1 tablespoon chives, chopped

½ cup peas
1 teaspoon whole-grain mustard
2 eggs
1 cup Panko bread crumbs
Vegetable oil for drizzling

### DIRECTIONS

1. In a large mixing bowl, add potatoes, salmon, scallions, lemon juice, parsley, chives, peas, mustard, and 1 egg (beaten). Mix until combined; mixture should still have a rough texture.

2. With an overflowing tablespoon of mixture, form a croquette—an oblong shape approximately 2 inches in length.

3. Make 19 croquettes and place on a baking tray; chill for at least 15 minutes.

4. While croquettes are chilling, preheat oven to 350°F.

5. In a shallow bowl, beat remaining egg. Place bread crumbs in another shallow dish.

6. Dip croquette in egg, coat in bread crumbs, and return to baking tray. Repeat for all croquettes.

7. Spray or lightly drizzle with vegetable oil. Place in oven for 20 minutes, until cooked through and golden.

8. Remove from oven and serve.

# ALASKA • AK

## Blueberry Meringue Pie

**LEVEL 3**
*Serves 8*

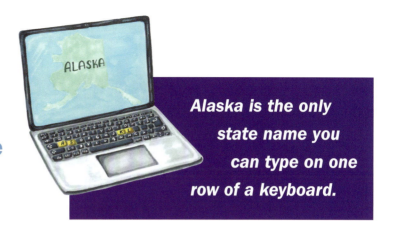

*Alaska is the only state name you can type on one row of a keyboard.*

### INGREDIENTS

#### CRUST

50 vanilla wafer cookies
3 tablespoons sugar
⅛ teaspoon kosher salt
5 tablespoons unsalted butter, melted

#### FILLING

One 2.9-ounce box cook-and-serve
  lemon pudding
3 egg yolks
¾ cup sugar
2¼ cups water

#### MERINGUE

2 tablespoons freeze-dried
  blueberry powder
  (make your own with one
  1.2-ounce bag freeze-dried
  blueberries, crushed in a blender
  or chopped to a fine powder)
1¾ cups sugar
⅔ cup water
6 large egg whites, room temperature
¼ teaspoon cream of tartar

### DIRECTIONS

#### CRUST

1. Preheat oven to 350°F.
2. Place wafers, sugar, and salt in a food processor and process to a fine crumb. Add melted butter and process for 30 seconds to incorporate.
3. Press crumbs evenly into a 9-inch pie pan.
4. Place in oven on center rack and bake for 10 minutes or until golden brown. (Start watching with the oven light after 8 minutes.)
5. Place on a rack to cool for 10 minutes before pouring in filling.

# ALASKA · AK

### FILLING

1. Follow instructions on pudding box.
2. When crust has cooled, pour hot pudding right into crust. Let cool to set up for at least 30 minutes before making meringue.

*What birthday party game do fish like to play? Salmon Says.*

### MERINGUE

1. In a small saucepan over medium heat, add blueberry powder, sugar, and water, stirring to dissolve sugar.
2. Attach a candy thermometer to pan. Make sure tip of thermometer is not touching base of pan. Cook until thermometer reads 240°F.
3. While sugar is cooking, in a large bowl (or stand mixer bowl) add room-temperature egg whites and cream of tartar. Using a mixer, bring egg whites to soft peak stage. Set aside.
4. When sugar mixture is ready, slowly drizzle it into egg whites while mixer is on medium speed. Once all of sugar mixture has been added, turn mixer to high and beat until glossy peaks are reached. Using a spatula, top pie with meringue.
5. This final step should be done by an adult. Place a single rack in the oven 12 inches from the broiler. Preheat broiler on high. Place pie on the rack and broil for 1 to 2 minutes.
6. Optional step: If the adult helping you has a crème brûlée torch, have them brown the top lightly with the torch; this meringue looks so pretty golden on top.

# CALIFORNIA • CA

## Avocado Toast

**LEVEL 1**

Serves 1

### INGREDIENTS

1 slice bread
½ ripe avocado
⅛ teaspoon salt
Extra toppings: fried egg sunny side up, cucumbers, scrambled egg and crispy bacon, tomato (optional)

### DIRECTIONS

1. Toast slice of bread until golden and firm.
2. Remove pit from avocado. Use a big spoon to scoop out the flesh. Put it in a bowl and mash it up with a fork until it's as smooth as you like it. Mix in a pinch of salt (about ⅛ teaspoon) and add more to taste, if desired.
3. Spread avocado on top of toast. Enjoy as is or top with additional toppings.

# CALIFORNIA • CA

## Fish Tacos

**LEVEL 2**

*Makes 24 small tacos*

> *What kind of fish eats mice?*
> *A catfish.*

### INGREDIENTS

½ teaspoon ground cumin

½ teaspoon cayenne pepper (optional)

1 teaspoon salt

¼ teaspoon black pepper

1½ pounds tilapia

1 tablespoon olive oil

1 tablespoon unsalted butter

24 small white corn tortillas

#### TACO SAUCE

½ cup sour cream

⅓ cup mayonnaise

2 tablespoons lime juice

1 teaspoon garlic powder

1 teaspoon sriracha (less if you don't want spicy)

#### TOPPINGS

½ small purple cabbage, chopped

2 Roma tomatoes, diced (optional)

½ red onion, diced

½ bunch cilantro, longer stems removed

4 ounces cotija cheese

1 lime cut into 8 wedges, to serve

### DIRECTIONS

1. Preheat oven to 375°F. Line a large baking sheet with parchment paper or a silicone liner.

2. In a small dish, combine cumin, cayenne pepper (if using), salt, and black pepper and evenly sprinkle seasoning mix over both sides of tilapia. Place on baking sheet.

3. Lightly drizzle fish with olive oil and dot each piece with butter. Bake for 20 to 25 minutes. To brown edges, broil for 3 to 5 minutes at the end if desired.

# CALIFORNIA · CA

4. In a medium bowl, whisk sour cream, mayonnaise, lime juice, garlic powder, and sriracha (if using) until well blended.

### ASSEMBLY

1. Quickly toast tortillas on a large, dry skillet or griddle over medium-high heat.
2. Fill a taco with pieces of fish, and then add cabbage, tomatoes, onion, and cilantro. Finish with a generous sprinkle of cotija cheese.
3. Serve with fresh lime wedges to squeeze over tacos.

> *The Redwood National and State Park forests have redwood trees so big cars can drive through them.*

# COLORADO • CO

## Denver Omelet

**LEVEL 2**

*Serves 4*

### INGREDIENTS

2 tablespoons butter

1 medium onion, chopped

1 red bell pepper, chopped

1 cup cooked ham, chopped

8 eggs

¼ cup milk

1 cup cheddar cheese, shredded

1 teaspoon salt

1 teaspoon pepper

### DIRECTIONS

1. Preheat oven to 400°F. Grease a round baking dish.
2. Melt butter in skillet over medium-low heat. Add onion and red pepper, and cook until soft. Add ham, and cook 2 minutes more.
3. Beat eggs and milk in a bowl. Stir in cheese and add ham mixture. Season with salt and pepper. Transfer to prepared dish.
4. Bake 20 minutes or until top is puffy and brown. Cut into wedges and serve warm.

# COLORADO · CO

*Two melons are on a date. One melon says, "Honeydew you love me?" The other melon replies, "Yes, but we cantaloupe."*

## Watermelon Sorbet

**LEVEL 1**
Serves 4

### INGREDIENTS

3½ cups fresh seedless watermelon chunks
2 teaspoons freshly squeezed lime juice
¼ cup warm water

### DIRECTIONS

1. Line a baking tray with parchment paper and place watermelon chunks on top of parchment. Place in freezer overnight.
2. Remove watermelon chunks from freezer and put in a blender, along with lime juice, and allow to sit for 5 minutes to slightly thaw.
3. Blend until smooth and add additional warm water to assist with blending.
4. Eat immediately or freeze in a freezer-safe container for 3 to 4 hours or until firm.

---

*One hundred fifty million years ago, part of Picket Wire Canyonlands was a large, shallow lake whose shoreline teemed with brontosaurs and allosaurs. Those epic creatures left footprints in the mud that eventually turned to stone. Today, over 1,300 of these footprints, extending on a quarter-mile plain, make up the largest dinosaur track in North America.*

# HAWAII • HI

## Roasted Pineapple Salsa

**LEVEL 2**

*Serves 6*

### INGREDIENTS

2 tablespoons extra-virgin olive oil
1 cup pineapple, cut into 2-inch chunks
2 heirloom tomatoes, diced
1 red onion, diced
1 garlic clove, minced
2 jalapeño peppers, seeds carefully removed, diced
½ cup cilantro leaves, chopped
Salt, to taste
Pepper, to taste

### DIRECTIONS

1. Heat olive oil in a skillet over medium-high heat and add pineapple chunks.
2. Cook for about 5 to 10 minutes, turning frequently to cook on all sides.
3. In a large bowl, add tomatoes, red onion, garlic, jalapeño, and cilantro. Mix together, and then season with salt and pepper. Drizzle with olive oil.
4. Remove pineapple from grill pan and chop into bite-size pieces. Fold into tomato mixture.

*What do you get when you cross an apple and a Christmas tree?*
*A pineapple.*

# HAWAII · HI

## Spam® Fries

**LEVEL 3**

*Serves 4*

### INGREDIENTS

One 12-ounce can Spam®
2 tablespoons extra-virgin olive oil
Vegetable oil for frying

**NOTE** More Spam® is consumed per person in Hawaii than in any other state in the United States. Almost 7 million cans of Spam® are eaten every year in Hawaii.

### DIRECTIONS

1. In a heavy, deep pan or fryer, heat 4 inches of oil at 350°F.
2. Cut Spam® into six even slices and then cut each slice into 4 matchsticks.
3. In small batches, place slices in hot oil. Fry 3 minutes or until golden brown and crisp.
4. Drain fries on paper towels.
5. Serve warm fries with ketchup or dipping sauce of your choice.

*Aloha, the Hawaiian word for love, affection, peace, compassion, and mercy, is commonly used as a simple greeting.*

# IDAHO · ID

## Huckleberry Pop Tarts

**LEVEL 3**

*Serves 6*

### INGREDIENTS

2 cups plus 2 tablespoons all-purpose flour, and additional for dusting
1 teaspoon coarse kosher salt
1 teaspoon sugar
1 cup unsalted butter, chilled, cut into ½-inch cubes
4 tablespoons ice water
1½ cups huckleberry jam
Confectioners' sugar for finishing (optional)

### DIRECTIONS

1. In a large bowl, whisk flour, salt, and sugar. Add butter and blend in until mixture resembles coarse meal. Add ice water by tablespoonfuls, tossing until moist clumps form.

2. Gather dough into ball. Divide in half; shape each half into disk. Wrap in plastic. Chill at least 1 hour.

3. Line 2 large, rimmed baking sheets with parchment paper.

4. Working with 1 disk at a time, roll out dough on floured surface to about 13 × 11 inches.

5. Trim to 12 × 10-inch rectangle, then cut into eight 3 × 5-inch rectangles.

6. Arrange 4 rectangles, spaced apart, on each sheet. Spoon 1½ tablespoons preserves down center of each rectangle. Top preserves with second dough rectangle.

# IDAHO • ID

7. Using fingertips, gently press all edges of each tart to seal; press all edges with tines of fork to double-seal. Using toothpick, poke a few holes in center of top dough rectangle. Cover; freeze tarts on sheets at least 2 hours and up to 1 week.

8. Position one rack in top third and one rack in bottom third of oven and preheat to 375°F. Bake frozen tarts uncovered until golden, reversing sheets after 15 minutes, 25 to 30 minutes total (some preserves may leak out). Immediately transfer tarts to cooling rack. Sift confectioners' sugar lightly over tarts, if desired.

9. Serve warm or at room temperature with fresh berries.

*The Boise State Broncos football team plays on a blue field, called Smurf turf.*

WEST 125

# IDAHO · ID

## Idaho Fries

**LEVEL 1**

*Serves 4*

### INGREDIENTS

4 Idaho potatoes, scrubbed
1 tablespoon olive oil or vegetable oil
1 teaspoon salt
1 teaspoon fresh ground pepper

### DIRECTIONS

1. Adjust oven rack to lowest position in oven. Preheat oven to 450°F.
2. Cut potatoes lengthwise into eighths to form wedges.
3. In a large bowl, toss potatoes with oil, salt, and pepper.
4. Arrange fries on a baking sheet flat in a single layer.
5. Bake potatoes without turning, until bottoms are golden and crisp, about 20 minutes. Flip potatoes to other side and bake 10 minutes more until crisp.
6. Remove from oven and sprinkle with more salt and pepper, to taste.

*How do you cheer up a baked potato? You butter him up.*

# MONTANA • MT

## Wheat Cinnamon Rolls

**LEVEL 3**

*Serves 16*

### INGREDIENTS

#### DOUGH

3¼ teaspoons dry yeast
¾ cup warm fat-free milk
¼ cup warm water
¼ cup butter, softened
¼ cup honey
½ teaspoon salt
1½ teaspoons fresh lemon juice
1 large egg
1 large egg white
2½ cups all-purpose flour
1½ cups whole wheat flour
Vegetable oil for coating

#### FILLING

¼ cup brown sugar, packed
1½ tablespoons ground cinnamon
⅛ teaspoon ground nutmeg
⅓ cup raisins (optional)

#### GLAZE

¾ cup confectioners' sugar, sifted
¾ teaspoon vanilla extract
5 teaspoons fat-free milk

### DIRECTIONS

1. In a large bowl, dissolve yeast in warm milk, add warm water, and let stand until bubbles form (approximately 5 minutes).
2. Add butter, honey, salt, lemon juice, egg, and egg white and stir well.
3. Add 2 cups all-purpose flour and whole wheat flour, mixing until a soft dough forms.
4. Flour a flat surface and knead dough until smooth and elastic, approximately 8 minutes. Add as needed the other ½ cup all-purpose flour.

# MONTANA • MT

5. Coat a large bowl with oil and add dough, turning it to cover all sides with oil. Cover and let rise in a warm place for 1 hour or until dough has doubled in size.

6. Flour a flat surface and roll dough out to a 6 × 12-inch rectangle. Coat surface of dough with oil.

7. For the filling, combine brown sugar, cinnamon, and nutmeg and sprinkle over dough, leaving a ½-inch border all around.

8. If you like, sprinkle raisins over dough and press down.

9. Roll up dough starting with the long edge of the rectangle.

10. Cut dough into 16 rolls.

11. Place rolls cut side up on a 13 × 9-inch greased baking pan.

12. Cover and let rise 45 minutes or until doubled in size.

13. Preheat oven to 375°F.

14. Uncover rolls. Bake for 22 minutes or until lightly browned. Cool in pan on a wire rack.

15. For glaze, in a small bowl, mix confectioners' sugar, vanilla extract, and milk.

16. Drizzle glaze evenly over rolls as they cool.

*What do you call a happy cowboy? A jolly rancher.*

# MONTANA • MT

## Beef Pasties

**LEVEL 3**

*Serves 4*

### INGREDIENTS

#### CRUST

2½ cups all-purpose flour
1 tablespoon sugar
1 teaspoon salt
2 cups unsalted butter,
    cut into ½-inch chunks
½ –⅔ cup buttermilk

#### FILLING

1 tablespoon unsalted butter
12 ounces beef chuck (stew meat),
    ½-inch dice
1½ cups potatoes, ½-inch dice
¾ cup carrots, ¼-inch dice

Water
1½ teaspoons salt
½ teaspoon crushed rosemary
¼ teaspoon pepper
¼ teaspoon oregano

#### GRAVY

3 tablespoons unsalted butter
½ cup onion, finely diced
2 tablespoons all-purpose flour

#### EGG WASH

1 egg
1 tablespoon milk

### DIRECTIONS

#### CRUST

1. In a large bowl, stir together flour, sugar, and salt. Pour into food processor. Add butter and pulse until butter is cut into flour mixture but still has visible chunks.

2. While pulsing, slowly pour in ½ cup buttermilk and continue to pulse until buttermilk is incorporated into the dough. Add more buttermilk if necessary. The dough should appear crumbly.

# MONTANA · MT

3. Lay a sheet of plastic wrap on the counter and place half of dough on the sheet. Fold plastic wrap around dough and press dough tightly together to form a 1-inch-thick disk. Repeat process with rest of dough. Place in a plastic bag and refrigerate for at least 1 hour, up to 24.

**NOTE** Montana pasties are a whole meal folded into a pastry shell—handheld and good to go.

### FILLING AND GRAVY

1. In a medium saucepan, melt butter over medium-high heat (watch closely, as you don't want to burn the butter) and add meat. Cook until well browned.

2. Add potatoes and carrots and cover with just enough water to submerge meat and vegetables. Add salt, rosemary, pepper, and oregano.

3. Bring to a boil, turn down to medium, and simmer for 5 minutes. Meat should be cooked through, and potatoes should be softened but still have a bit of stiffness.

4. Remove from heat and drain cooking liquid into a separate container for later use. Set liquid and meat and vegetables aside.

5. In a medium saucepan, melt remaining 3 tablespoons butter over medium heat. Add onions and cook until they begin to soften, about 2 to 3 minutes. Add flour and whisk continuously for 1 minute until a sticky paste forms and flour turns golden. Whisk in 1 cup of reserved cooking liquid from meat and potatoes (discard the rest). Simmer for 2 to 4 minutes, whisking continuously, until a thick gravy forms. Remove from heat and stir in meat and vegetable mixture, making sure everything is well coated.

# MONTANA · MT

**ASSEMBLY**

1. Preheat oven to 400°F. Use a silicone mat or lightly grease baking sheet.
2. In a small bowl, whisk together egg and milk to create an egg wash.
3. On a well-floured flat surface, divide dough into 4 to 6 equal-size pieces and roll into balls. Re-flour your work surface and with a floured rolling pin roll first ball out to 3/8 inch thick, forming as round a circle as you can manage (trim edges with a knife if necessary). Pick up your dough to make sure it is not stuck to your work surface. If it is, use a metal spatula to dislodge it before filling.
4. Brush egg wash around edges of dough to help seal it and spoon meat mixture over slightly less than half of dough, leaving a ½-inch border. Fold dough over filling and use a fork to crimp edges closed. Cut 3 slashes in the top and transfer to baking pan.
5. Repeat with remaining dough balls. You may have a bit of meat mixture left over, depending on how thin you rolled out your dough.
6. Brush pasties with egg wash and bake for 15 to 20 minutes, until they are golden and puffed.
7. Allow to cool slightly prior to serving.

*The largest snowflake ever observed was seen in Fort Keogh, Montana. This snowflake had an incredible diameter of 15 inches.*

# NEVADA • NV

## Onion Rings

**LEVEL 3**

*Serves 6*

### INGREDIENTS

1 large Vidalia or other sweet onion
1 quart oil for frying
1¼ cups all-purpose flour
1 teaspoon baking powder
1 teaspoon salt

1 cup milk
1 large egg
¾ cup bread crumbs
⅛ teaspoon salt, or to taste

### DIRECTIONS

1. Slice onion into ¼-inch-thick rings.
2. Heat oil in a deep fryer or deep skillet to 365°F. Place a wire rack over a sheet of aluminum foil.
3. Prepare breading station by setting out three wide, shallow dishes. Stir flour, baking powder, and salt together in the first dish. Whisk milk and egg together in the second dish. Place bread crumbs in the third dish.
4. Dip onion ring into flour mixture, turning several times until fully coated with flour. Transfer to egg mixture and use a fork to turn until coated. Lift onion with the fork and shake gently so excess liquid drips back into the dish. Place onion in bread crumbs and turn several times to coat, scooping crumbs over the ring if necessary. Lift again with the fork, tap any excess bread crumbs back into the dish, and place on the wire rack. Prepare remaining onion rings.
5. Deep-fry 3 to 4 onion rings at a time in the preheated oil until golden brown, 2 to 3 minutes. Drain on paper towels while you deep-fry remaining rings.
6. Sprinkle with salt before serving.

# NEVADA · NV

*In 1873, the Reno-based tailor Jacob Davis teamed up with Levi Strauss, and together they invented the first pair of blue jeans.*

## Shrimp Cocktail

**LEVEL 1**

*Serves 8 to 9*

### INGREDIENTS

**SHRIMP**

- 2 pounds ice
- 6 cups water, plus more to cover ice
- 2 lemons
- 2 tablespoons kosher salt
- 2 tablespoons sugar
- ½ small onion, peeled and halved
- 1 small bunch parsley
- 2 pounds shrimp, peeled and deveined

**COCKTAIL SAUCE**

- ½ cup mild chili sauce
- ½ cup ketchup
- 1 teaspoon lemon zest
- 2 tablespoons fresh lemon juice
- 1 tablespoon horseradish
- 1 teaspoon Worcestershire sauce
- ¼ teaspoon celery salt
- 2 dashes hot sauce (optional)

### DIRECTIONS

1. Fill a large bowl halfway with ice and add water to cover; set aside. Cut 1 lemon into wedges.

2. In a large pot, combine 6 cups water, salt, sugar, onion, and 5 sprigs parsley. Halve and juice remaining lemon and add to pot. Bring to a boil, and then turn off heat and add shrimp to pot. Let sit until shrimp are pink and cooked through, about 3 minutes. Remove shrimp from pot and add to the bowl of ice.

3. In a small bowl, make cocktail sauce by mixing chili sauce, ketchup, lemon zest, lemon juice, horseradish, Worcestershire sauce, celery salt, and hot sauce (if using).

4. Garnish shrimp with parsley and serve with lemon wedges and cocktail sauce.

*How do you make a shrimp laugh? Tell a whale of a tale.*

# OREGON • OR

## Blueberry Hazelnut Breakfast Cookies

**LEVEL 2**

*Makes 12 cookies*

### INGREDIENTS

1 cup hazelnuts
½ cup whole wheat flour
1½ cups old-fashioned rolled oats
1½ teaspoons ground cinnamon
1 teaspoon baking soda
¼ teaspoon fine sea salt
2 medium ripe bananas

1 egg
⅓ cup honey or maple syrup
¼ cup coconut oil, melted
1 teaspoon vanilla extract
Finely grated zest of 1 lemon
1 cup fresh or frozen blueberries

### DIRECTIONS

1. Preheat oven to 350°F. Line a large baking sheet with parchment paper.

2. On a medium baking sheet, scatter hazelnuts. Roast until fragrant and skins are blistered, 12 to 15 minutes. Let cool slightly, then transfer ½ cup hazelnuts to a food processor along with the flour. Pulse until hazelnuts are ground into a fine flour. Roughly chop remaining hazelnuts and set aside.

3. In a large bowl, add hazelnut-flour mixture with oats, cinnamon, baking soda, and salt. Stir to combine.

4. In a large bowl, mash bananas. Stir in egg, honey or maple syrup, oil, vanilla extract, and lemon zest until smooth. Stir in oat mixture until thoroughly combined. Fold in chopped hazelnuts and blueberries.

5. Pack cookie mixture into a ⅓-cup measure, and then tap measuring cup onto lined baking sheet so cookies fall out in rounds. Flatten each cookie slightly.

6. Bake until browned and set, 15 to 18 minutes. Let cool completely on baking sheet.

# OREGON · OR

## Almond Butter and Nut Pear Wedges

**LEVEL 1**
*Serves 4*

### INGREDIENTS

1 large pear, quartered, cored, cut into wedges
⅓ cup almond, Brazil, or cashew spread
½ cup finely chopped nuts of your choice: walnuts, pecans, or peanuts

### DIRECTIONS

1. Spread nut butter on half of each pear wedge and sprinkle with chopped nuts.
2. Serve immediately.

**TIP** Swap out almond butter with peanut butter or Nutella®

*What are the two things you can't have for breakfast?
Lunch and dinner!*

**The World's Smallest Park is in the middle of Portland. Mill Ends Park is a circle two feet across, with a total area of 452 square inches and one very small tree.**

WEST

# UTAH • UT

## Pineapple Cucumber Lime Jell-O® Salad

**LEVEL 2**

Serves 8

### INGREDIENTS

One 6-ounce package Jell-O® lime gelatin
1 teaspoon salt
2 cups hot water
2 cups cold water
1½ cups cucumbers, peeled and diced
1½ cups canned pineapple, drained
3 tablespoons horseradish
½ teaspoon grated onion
2 tablespoons vinegar

*Jell-O® is Utah's official state food. Utah has historically consumed more Jell-O® per capita than any other state in the nation.*

### DIRECTIONS

1. In a medium bowl, dissolve lime Jell-O® and salt in 2 cups hot (not boiling) water. Add 2 cups cold water and chill until slightly thickened, approximately 30 minutes.

2. In another bowl, mix cucumbers, pineapple, horseradish, grated onion, and vinegar. Fold pineapple and cucumber mixture into Jell-O® and pour into a Jell-O® mold. Refrigerate for a minimum of 6 hours until set.

3. To remove Jell-O® from its mold, fill up a basin halfway with hot water. Lower the Jell-O® mold into the hot water, metal side down, until water comes up to the edge of the mold. Keep it there 5 minutes. Place a plate on top of the mold and turn upside down. The Jell-O® salad should simply slide out.

**TIP** You cannot use fresh pineapple with gelatin. The bromelain enzyme in the fruit will keep gelatin from bonding.

# UTAH · UT

## Potato Casserole

**LEVEL 1**
*Serves 12*

*Where do baby apes sleep? In apricots.*

### INGREDIENTS

30 ounces frozen hash browns, defrosted
2 cups sour cream
One 10.5-ounce can cream of chicken soup
10 tablespoons butter, melted
1 teaspoon salt
¼ teaspoon freshly ground black pepper
1 teaspoon dried minced onion
2 cups shredded cheddar cheese
2 cups cornflakes cereal

### DIRECTIONS

1. Allow potatoes to thaw in fridge overnight or spread them on a baking sheet and warm them in oven at 200°F for about 20 minutes, until thawed.
2. Preheat oven to 350°F.
3. Combine sour cream, cream of chicken soup, 6 tablespoons melted butter, salt, pepper, and dried onion in a bowl. Mix well.
4. Add potatoes and shredded cheese and stir to combine. Spoon mixture into a single layer in a 9 × 13-inch pan.
5. Put cornflakes in a large resealable bag and crush gently with your hands or a rolling pin. Pour in a bowl.
6. Add remaining 4 tablespoons melted butter to crushed cornflakes and combine well. Sprinkle mixture over potatoes.
7. Bake uncovered at 350°F for 40 to 50 minutes.

# WASHINGTON • WA

## Wild Mushroom Barley

**LEVEL 2**

*Serves 2 to 4*

### INGREDIENTS

1 cup barley
2 cups water
1 tablespoon olive oil
8 ounces wild mushrooms (oyster, portobello, shiitake, cremini), sliced
2 garlic cloves, minced
1 ounce baby spinach
¼ cup parsley, chopped
2 tablespoons chives, minced
1 teaspoon kosher salt
½ teaspoon black pepper

### DIRECTIONS

1. In a medium saucepan, combine barley and water. Bring to a boil, reduce heat, and simmer for 12 minutes until barley is tender. Let stand for 2 to 3 minutes and fluff with a fork.

2. In a large skillet, heat olive oil over medium-high heat. Add mushrooms and sauté for 5 minutes until mushrooms start to brown. Stir in garlic and continue cooking for a few minutes until mushrooms are caramelized and fragrant.

3. Fold barley into mushroom mixture and then add spinach, letting leaves wilt. Stir in parsley, chives, salt, and pepper.

4. Serve hot or cold.

*Longview has several bridges made for squirrels, the first one made in 1963 by Amos Peters, who wanted to help the animals cross the street safely.*

# WASHINGTON • WA

## Emma's Applesauce

**LEVEL 1**

*Serves 4*

### INGREDIENTS

3 pounds (about 6 medium) apples, peeled, cored, and chopped

⅓ cup water

2–4 tablespoons sugar, or to taste

¼ teaspoon ground cinnamon

### DIRECTIONS

1. In a medium saucepan, combine apples, water, sugar, and cinnamon and bring to a boil.

2. Cook 15 to 20 minutes or until apples are very tender. Remove lid and simmer an additional 5 minutes to thicken.

3. Mash apples with a masher for a chunky consistency or blend/puree with an immersion blender for a smooth consistency.

4. Serve warm or chilled.

*What did the apple skin say to the apple?*

*I got you covered.*

# WYOMING · WY

## Wyoming Stew

**LEVEL 2**

*Serves 8*

### INGREDIENTS

1 pound beef stew meat, cubed
2 teaspoons meat tenderizer
One 14.5-ounce can chicken broth
One 10.75-ounce can condensed cream of chicken soup
1 packet dry onion soup mix
16 ounces frozen mixed vegetables
1 can crescent dinner rolls

The bison is the official state mammal.

### DIRECTIONS

1. Sprinkle meat tenderizer over beef cubes.
2. In a cast-iron skillet over medium-high heat, cook beef cubes until browned. Drain excess grease.
3. In a small bowl, mix together chicken broth, cream of chicken soup, and onion soup mix. Pour over beef, reduce heat to low, and simmer for 45 minutes.
4. Preheat oven to 350°F.
5. Add frozen vegetables to skillet and simmer for 10 minutes.
6. Unroll crescent roll dough, and arrange dough to cover the top of the pan like a pie.
7. Bake for 10 to 15 minutes or until top is golden brown.
8. Remove from oven and serve.

*What did the buffalo say when his son left to go to school?*
*Bison.*

# WYOMING · WY

## Wyoming Cowboy Cookies

**LEVEL 2**

*Makes 12 cookies*

### INGREDIENTS

½ cup coconut, shredded

6 tablespoons pecans, chopped

½ cup butter, melted

¾ cup brown sugar

1 large egg

¾ teaspoon vanilla extract

1 cup all-purpose flour

½ teaspoon baking soda

¼ teaspoon sea salt

1 cup old-fashioned oats

1 cup chocolate chips

### DIRECTIONS

1. Preheat oven to 350°F. Line 2 baking sheets with parchment paper.
2. Place shredded coconut and pecans on a baking sheet and bake for 6 minutes or until toasted, moving around halfway through.
3. In a large bowl, using a mixer, cream butter and sugar until light and fluffy.
4. Add egg and vanilla extract and beat together.
5. In another bowl, combine flour, baking soda, and salt. Add this dry mixture to wet mixture and stir until well combined.
6. Stir in oats, chocolate chips, and toasted coconut and pecans.
7. Using an ice cream scooper, drop cookie batter onto baking sheets 2 inches apart. Bake for 12 minutes.

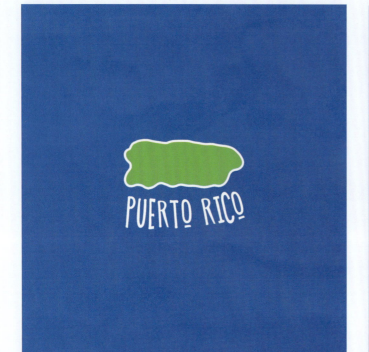

# THE FEDERAL DISTRICT, AMERICAN COMMONWEALTHS, AND TERRITORIES

## WASHINGTON, D.C.

**Washington, D.C.**
The Federal District,
known as District of Columbia . . . **144**

## COMMONWEALTHS

**Puerto Rico (Caribbean)** . . . **146**

**Northern Mariana Islands (Pacific)** . . . **150**

## TERRITORIES

**Guam (Pacific)** . . . **153**

**American Samoa (Pacific)** . . . **155**

**US Virgin Islands (Caribbean)**
The three main islands are
St. Thomas, St. Croix, and St. John . . . **157**

# WASHINGTON, D.C.

## Senate Bean Soup

**LEVEL 2**

Serves 10 to 12

### INGREDIENTS

1 pound dried navy beans
4 cups hot water
2 tablespoons olive oil
1 medium yellow onion, finely chopped
1 large carrot, finely chopped
1 celery stalk, finely chopped
8 ounces thick-cut cooked ham, diced
2 garlic cloves, finely chopped
2 bay leaves
2 teaspoons ground black pepper
1 teaspoon kosher salt
½ teaspoon dried thyme
½ teaspoon dried rosemary
6 cups low-sodium chicken broth
2 tablespoons unsalted butter

### DIRECTIONS

1. Rinse beans, removing and discarding damaged or discolored ones. In a large pot, combine hot water and beans. Bring to a boil over medium-high heat. Boil for 2 minutes, and then remove pot from heat. Cover and let soak for 1 hour.

2. When beans are done soaking, pour through a colander to drain. Wipe pot clean.

3. In the same pot, heat olive oil over medium heat until shimmering. Add onion, carrot, and celery, and cook, stirring occasionally, until fragrant and beginning to soften, about 3 minutes. Add ham, garlic, bay leaves, pepper, salt, thyme, and rosemary. Sauté until fragrant, about 1 minute.

4. Add beans and stir to combine. Add chicken broth and bring to a boil over high heat. Reduce heat to medium-low and simmer, stirring occasionally, until beans are tender, 1 hour 30 minutes to 1 hour 45 minutes.

5. Add unsalted butter and stir until melted. Taste and season with more salt as needed.

*What do ducks put in their soup? Quackers.*

144 RECIPE ROAD TRIP

# WASHINGTON, D.C.

## Mambo Sauce

**LEVEL 1**

*Makes 28 tablespoons*

### INGREDIENTS

¾ cup ketchup
½ cup white vinegar
¼ cup soy sauce
¼ cup sugar (or more, if you like sweeter)
1 tablespoon cayenne

**TIP** For a milder taste, replace cayenne with paprika.

### DIRECTIONS

1. In a medium pot, whisk together ketchup, vinegar, soy sauce, sugar, and cayenne.

2. Heat to medium and cook, stirring for 10 minutes to combine flavors. Remove from heat.

3. Cool and serve, or store in the refrigerator in an airtight container.

> All US presidents except one, George Washington, have lived and worked in the White House. The original name of the building was the President's Palace or the President's House. After the name appeared in a newspaper article in 1901, President Theodore Roosevelt made the name change official.

THE FEDERAL DISTRICT, AMERICAN COMMONWEALTHS, AND TERRITORIES   145

# PUERTO RICO

## Empanadillas (Puerto Rican Fried Turnovers)

**LEVEL 3**

*Makes 10 to 12 empanadillas*

### INGREDIENTS

#### DOUGH

2 cups all-purpose flour
½ teaspoon salt
¼ cup butter, melted
2 egg yolks
½ cup water

#### PICADILLO FILLING

1 teaspoon olive oil
1 yellow onion, diced
1 red bell pepper, diced
1 cup sofrito (see facing page)
1 pound lean ground beef
1 teaspoon sazón seasoning
1 teaspoon adobo seasoning
3 bay leaves
One 15-ounce can tomato sauce
⅓ cup pimento-stuffed olives, sliced in half
¼ cup water
Salt, to taste
½ cup vegetable oil for frying

*El Yunque National Forest, in northeastern Puerto Rico, is the only tropical rainforest in the United States' national forest system. Its 29,000 acres make it one of the smallest forests in the country. Despite its size, it is impressive, with mountains over 3,000 feet in height and exotic wildlife.*

# PUERTO RICO

### DIRECTIONS

1. Make dough (skip this step if using store-bought dough). Combine all ingredients in a bowl and mix well until a ball begins to form. Dust a flat surface with flour and knead dough until no longer sticky. Chill for 30 minutes while you make filling.

2. Make picadillo filling. In a pan over medium heat, add oil, onion, and pepper. Once onions become clear, add sofrito and sauté another minute before adding ground beef. With a spatula, break ground beef into smaller pieces while it cooks. Add sazón, adobo, bay leaves, tomato sauce, olives, and water. Bring to a boil before simmering with a lid partially on for 10 minutes, or until beef is fully cooked. Taste and add salt, if necessary.

3. Prep dough. Dust a flat surface with flour and divide dough into 10 or 12 circular disks (depending on yield). Spoon picadillo filling on one half of each disk and fold empty dough side over filling and seal edges with a fork.

4. Heat oil around 350°F and fry empanadillas 4 minutes per side; they should be golden brown and crispy at the edges.

## Sofrito

### LEVEL 1
1 yellow onion, chopped
1 green bell pepper, chopped
4 garlic cloves, chopped
1 cup cilantro, chopped
1 jalapeño, seeds removed, chopped (optional)

In a food processor, combine all ingredients and pulse until a consistent mix is formed. Store in the refrigerator for up to 2 weeks. Use as a base for savory dishes.

# PUERTO RICO

## Tostones (Fried Green Plantains)

**LEVEL 3**

*Serves 8*

### INGREDIENTS

4 green plantains
1 cup vegetable or canola oil
2 cups water
4 cloves garlic, minced
1 tablespoon kosher salt, plus more to top
1 lime, juiced
Mojo verde sauce, for serving (see facing page)

### DIRECTIONS

1. For each plantain, cut off ends and then cut through skin lengthwise, from top to bottom.

2. Pry open and peel off tough outer skin. Discard.

3. Cut plantains into pieces, about 1 inch thick.

4. Fill a large, heavy-bottomed skillet about a third of the way with oil. Heat over medium for a few minutes to warm up oil.

5. In a large bowl, combine water, garlic, salt, and lime juice. Set aside.

6. Add plantain slices to oil, which should be warm enough to lightly bubble after plantains are added. Fry plantains until softened and golden all over, about 4 minutes on each side. Use tongs to transfer to a paper towel–lined plate.

7. Using the bottom of a glass plate or can, gently flatten each fried plantain. Smash just enough to flatten out.

## PUERTO RICO

*What kind of fruit is the craziest to eat? A plantain—it's just bananas!*

8. Dip flattened plantain in the garlic-lime water. Let it sit for 10 seconds, and then remove from water and gently pat dry with a paper towel. Repeat with remaining fried plantains.

9. When about to serve, heat oil over medium-high heat. Add flattened plantains back into oil in batches and briefly fry to crisp, about 1 minute per side. Remove with tongs and transfer to a paper towel–lined plate.

10. Sprinkle with salt and serve with mojo verde or other sauces, if desired.

### Mojo Verde

**LEVEL 1**

1 large bunch cilantro, leaves and tender stems only
4 large garlic cloves, peeled
2 limes, juiced
½ teaspoon cumin
1 tablespoon white wine vinegar
½ cup olive oil
Kosher salt, to taste

> Mojo is an uncooked, fresh, and vibrant sauce that's used as a condiment, a topping, or a marinade for fish, chicken, vegetables, and more.

In the bowl of a food processor or blender, combine cilantro, garlic, lime juice, cumin, white vinegar, and olive oil. Process until well combined. Season generously with kosher salt and serve immediately, or cover and refrigerate until ready to use.

# NORTHERN MARIANA ISLANDS

## Coconut Rice

**LEVEL 1**

*Makes four ½-cup servings*

### INGREDIENTS

1 cup jasmine, basmati, or long-grain white rice

1 cup light coconut milk

1 cup water or coconut water

¼ teaspoon sea salt

2 tablespoons unsweetened shredded coconut (optional, for more coconut flavor and texture)

Cilantro, finely minced, for garnish (optional)

¼ teaspoon lightly toasted coconut flakes, for garnish (optional)

### DIRECTIONS

1. In a large saucepan, add rice, coconut milk, water or coconut water, sea salt, and shredded coconut (if using), and bring to a boil over high heat. Once boiling, lower heat to a simmer and cover. Ensure it's simmering and not boiling or the rice will cook too quickly.

2. Simmer until water is completely absorbed and rice is tender, about 20 to 25 minutes.

3. Turn off heat, remove lid, fluff rice with a fork, put lid back on, and let rest for 10 minutes so moisture redistributes, preventing mushy rice. Taste test and add more salt if desired.

4. Garnish with cilantro and coconut flakes, if desired.

*Why do bananas never get lonely? Because they hang out in bunches.*

RECIPE ROAD TRIP

# NORTHERN MARIANA ISLANDS

## Rosketti

**LEVEL 2**

*Makes 30 to 36 cookies*

### INGREDIENTS

1 cup butter, softened
⅔ cup sugar
3 eggs, beaten
2 teaspoons vanilla extract
4 cups cornstarch
2½ cups flour
1 tablespoon baking powder
¼ teaspoon salt

### DIRECTIONS

1. Preheat oven to 350°F.
2. In a medium bowl, beat butter until smooth.
3. While continuing to beat, slowly add sugar and beat until mixture is creamy.
4. Gradually incorporate eggs while beating.
5. Stir in vanilla extract.
6. In a separate bowl, sift cornstarch, flour, baking powder, and salt.
7. Add dry ingredients to creamy mixture, stirring until well combined and mixture is smooth.
8. Line 2 baking sheets with parchment paper.
9. Divide dough into 30 to 36 pieces and form smooth balls the size of a ping-pong ball.

# NORTHERN MARIANA ISLANDS

**10.** Shape cookies. Create both shapes or just one—or design your own!

**a. First shape:** Place balls, well spaced, on baking sheet. Press each ball with a fork, flattening it and making it slightly oval.

**b. Second shape:** Form a rope with each ball and then wrap it around itself, making a snail shape. Place on baking sheet.

**11.** Bake rosketti for 15 to 20 minutes. Edges should turn golden brown and rest of cookies remain very light. Remove from oven and place on a wire rack to cool.

**TIP** These delicious shortbread cookies can be made into many different shapes, including a pretzel. This recipe features two traditional shapes.

The Mariana region contains nine volcanic islands and more than sixty submarine volcanoes, of which at least twenty are hydrothermally active. The summits of these submarine volcanoes range from 50 meters to more than 1,800 meters below sea level. This is one of the most active volcanic regions on Earth.

152 RECIPE ROAD TRIP

# GUAM

## Buñelos Aga (Banana Doughnuts)

**LEVEL 3**

Makes 10 to 12 doughnuts

### INGREDIENTS

Vegetable oil for frying
2 cups mashed ripe bananas
2 cups flour
½ teaspoon baking powder
¼ cup sugar
⅛ teaspoon salt
1 teaspoon cinnamon
1 teaspoon vanilla extract
2 tablespoons milk
Maple syrup for dipping or glazing

### DIRECTIONS

1. To preheat oil, place in a large frying pan and turn heat to medium. Cover a baking sheet with paper towels and set aside.

2. In a large bowl, thoroughly mix bananas, flour, baking powder, sugar, salt, cinnamon, vanilla extract, and milk. The mixture will look like mashed bananas, but firmer, because of the flour. The batter will be very sticky.

3. When oil is hot, drop batter by spoonful into the oil, turning frequently.

4. Deep-fry over medium heat. If oil is too hot, doughnuts will burn on the outside before the inside cooks. Cook until golden brown.

5. With a slotted spoon, carefully remove doughnuts from pan and place on prepared plate.

6. Serve warm with a side of maple syrup for dipping, or glaze all the doughnuts with maple syrup.

*A man goes to the doctor with a banana in one ear, a carrot in the other ear, and a cucumber up his nose. "What's wrong with me, Doc?" he asks.*

*"It's easy," the doctor replies. "You're just not eating properly."*

153

# GUAM

## Cucumber Salad

**LEVEL 1**

*Serves 4*

### INGREDIENTS

2 large cucumbers
2 tablespoons salt
¼ cup onions, finely chopped
⅛ teaspoon black pepper
¼ cup soy sauce
2 tablespoons white vinegar

### DIRECTIONS

1. Slice cucumbers about ¼ inch thick. Place cucumber slices in a plastic colander and then place colander in a large bowl. Sprinkle salt over cucumbers and stir to combine. Let salted cucumber slices sit for about 15 minutes to allow excess water to drain out. After 15 minutes, pour out any water that drained into the bowl. Rinse salt off cucumbers and drain.

2. Place rinsed and drained cucumber slices in the large bowl. Add onion, pepper, soy sauce, and vinegar. Stir to combine.

3. Let cucumbers sit for several minutes to soak up all of the flavors. A longer time will enhance flavors.

4. Serve in the bowl.

---

*Found nowhere else on Earth, Guam's national bird, the Guam rail—also known as the ko'ko'—had been extinct in the wild for almost forty years. But in 2019, it was successfully reintroduced into the wild and is now classified as critically endangered. It's only the second bird in history to recover from extinction in the wild.*

# AMERICAN SAMOA

## Palusami

**LEVEL 3**

*Serves 4*

### INGREDIENTS

12 ounces corned beef
1 yellow onion, diced
2 garlic cloves, chopped
Salt and pepper, to taste
14 leaves Swiss chard, stems removed
15 ounces coconut cream

**NOTE** This family favorite is made with taro leaves. Since they are hard to find, this recipe has been modified to use Swiss chard.

### DIRECTIONS

1. Preheat oven to 350°F.
2. In a large mixing bowl, add corned beef, onion, garlic, salt, and pepper. Stir to combine.
3. Wash and dry Swiss chard. On a sheet of aluminum foil, put 2 leaves on top of each other.
4. Scoop 3 tablespoons of corned beef mixture and place in the middle of top leaf. Drizzle coconut cream on top of filling, as well as on the leaf.
5. Fold each side of the leaf in and drizzle more coconut cream in between the 2 leaves. Fold all leaves to close up.
6. Keeping the palusami closed, wrap the aluminum foil around and seal. Repeat until you are out of leaves or filling, whichever comes first.
7. Bake for 30 minutes. Remove from oven and allow to cool before opening foil. Cool 10 minutes before serving.

# AMERICAN SAMOA

## Samoan Poi

**LEVEL 2**

*Serves 4*

### INGREDIENTS

4 bananas, peeled
½ cup coconut cream or milk
2 teaspoons sugar
½ teaspoon vanilla extract
Zest of ½ lemon

*How do you know the ocean is friendly? It waves.*

### DIRECTIONS

1. In a medium bowl, place bananas and mash with a fork.
2. Add coconut cream or milk, sugar, vanilla, and lemon zest.
3. If you want poi to be creamier, mix in a blender. Serve immediately.

*The movie* Moana *draws inspiration from the Samoan culture and language. For example, the film's houses are like a traditional Samoan* fale *(house).*

# US VIRGIN ISLANDS

## Fungi

**LEVEL 3**

*Serves 12 as side dish*

### INGREDIENTS

1 whole coconut
3½ cups water
2 cups cornmeal
Vegetable oil
1 cup okra, chopped
2 pimiento peppers, chopped
½ teaspoon black pepper
½ teaspoon chili pepper
1 teaspoon salt

½ medium onion, chopped
3 garlic cloves, grated
1 medium carrot, chopped
1 celery stalk, chopped
2 thyme branches, stem removed
1 bandhania leaf
　　(or substitute cilantro)
½ cup butter

### DIRECTIONS

1. Wrap coconut with cloth. Carefully break shell with a hammer.
2. Scrape out coconut flesh. Cut flesh into smaller pieces and wash.
3. Blend coconut with 2 cups water.
4. Strain coconut milk. Squeeze excess solid through a strainer. Discard solid.
5. Add cornmeal to a bowl. Add 1½ cups water and mix.
6. Add enough oil to cover the bottom of a large pot. Heat oil on medium heat.

**NOTE** Fungi (pronounced foon-gee) is not a mushroom. It is a tender, polenta-like dumpling prepared from salted cornmeal mixed with shortening and water. Scoops of fungi are usually served with generous portions of fish fillets or meat.

# US VIRGIN ISLANDS

7. Add okra, peppers, black pepper, chili pepper, salt, onion, garlic, carrot, celery, thyme, and bandhania to the hot oil. Sauté until okra is very soft before moving on to the next step.

8. Add coconut milk. Turn heat to high to allow it to boil and then immediately let it simmer.

9. While mixture is simmering, add cornmeal spoon by spoon while continually mixing. Mixture will begin to clump.

10. Add butter and mix in completely.

11. After 10 minutes of mixing, add to a baking dish. Spread it out evenly. Allow it to sit and cool for 10 minutes to harden.

*What do you call a coconut that doesn't have milk? A milk dud.*

**NOTE** The festival of Carnival is celebrated across the Caribbean with steel drum bands, colorful costumes that can take months to prepare, and parades. Each island celebrates Carnival at a different time of the year: St. Thomas celebrates after Easter, St. John around the Fourth of July, and St. Croix during the week between Christmas and New Year's Day.

# US VIRGIN ISLANDS

## Callaloo

**LEVEL 2**

*Serves 4*

### INGREDIENTS

3 tablespoons butter or olive oil
1 sweet onion, peeled and chopped
1 red bell pepper, seeded and chopped
1 large tomato, cut into 4 wedges
1 cup scallions, chopped
3–4 garlic cloves, minced

1 teaspoon dried thyme
2 cups vegetable broth
1 teaspoon salt
½ teaspoon pepper
16 cups fresh callaloo, roughly chopped

### DIRECTIONS

1. In a large 6- to 8-quart pot over medium heat, add butter, onion, bell pepper, and sauté for 2 to 3 minutes. Add in tomato, scallions, and garlic. Sauté 3 to 4 minutes to soften.

2. Add thyme, broth, salt, and pepper. Stir well.

3. Begin adding callaloo to the pot. Gradually add handfuls of greens, and as they wilt down, continue adding until all greens have been cooked down in the pot. Cover and simmer on medium-low for 30 to 45 minutes, stirring occasionally.

4. Taste and add salt and pepper as needed. Serve warm.

**TIP** Substitute a blend of half fresh spinach leaves and half collard greens for callaloo leaves.

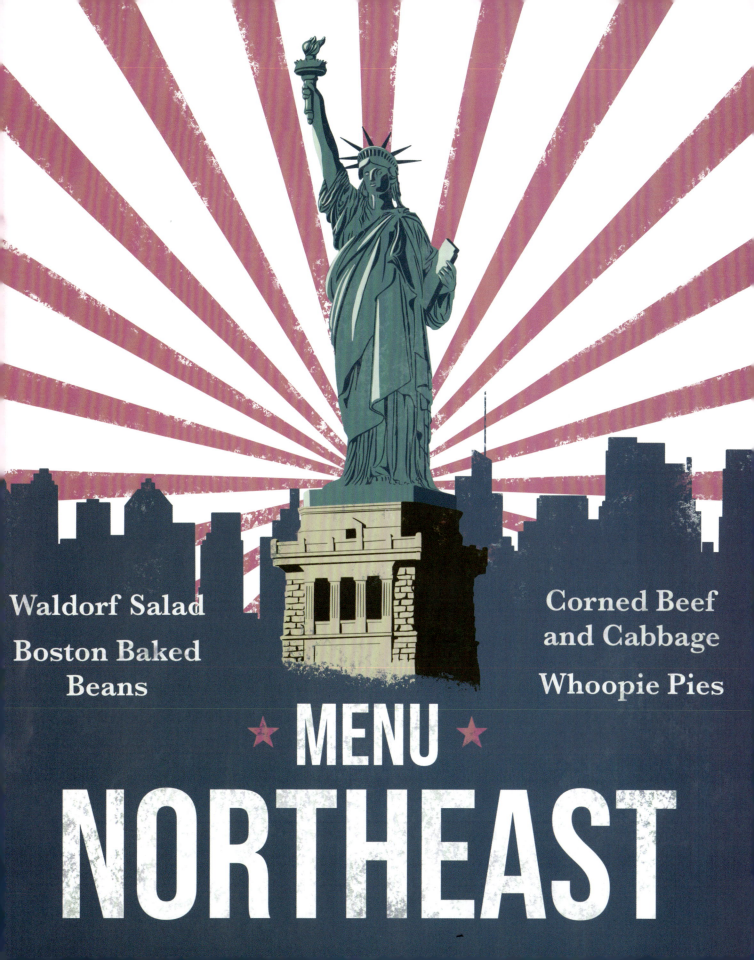

# NORTHEAST MENU

## Waldorf Salad

**LEVEL 1**

*Serves 2*

### INGREDIENTS

2 large Gala or Honeycrisp apples, unpeeled and chopped

2 cups chopped celery

¼ cup raisins

¼ cup walnuts, toasted

⅓ cup reduced-fat mayonnaise

⅓ cup plain yogurt

### DIRECTIONS

In a large bowl, combine apples, celery, raisins, and walnuts. Add mayonnaise and yogurt; toss to coat. Refrigerate, covered, until serving.

# NORTHEAST MENU

## Boston Baked Beans

**LEVEL 2**

*Serves 6 to 8*

### INGREDIENTS

8 ounces bacon (7 to 8 slices), cut into ½-inch pieces
1 medium onion, finely chopped
5 garlic cloves, minced
2 tablespoons brown sugar
⅓ cup molasses
One 15-ounce can diced tomatoes
⅓ cup ketchup
2 tablespoons Worcestershire sauce
2 tablespoons yellow mustard
2 teaspoons paprika
2 bay leaves
½ teaspoon black pepper
½ teaspoon cloves, ground
1 teaspoon kosher salt
Three 15-ounce cans navy beans, drained

### DIRECTIONS

1. Preheat oven to 325°F.
2. Heat a 6-quart Dutch oven over medium heat. Add bacon and cook until crisp and fat is rendered, 7 to 10 minutes. Transfer bacon to a bowl using a slotted spoon.
3. Add onions and garlic to bacon fat in pot and sauté until soft and translucent, about 5 minutes. Add brown sugar, molasses, tomatoes, ketchup, Worcestershire sauce, mustard, paprika, bay leaves, pepper, cloves, salt, navy beans, and reserved bacon to the pot.
4. Over medium-high heat, bring mixture to a simmer, stirring frequently. Cover pot with lid and transfer to the oven. Bake until sauce has thickened, 45 to 55 minutes. Check beans and stir once halfway through cooking time.
5. Let beans rest out of the oven for 10 minutes before serving. Garnish with extra bacon if desired.

# NORTHEAST MENU

## Corned Beef and Cabbage

**LEVEL 2**

*Serves 8*

### INGREDIENTS

One 3½-pound corned beef brisket or fresh beef brisket

15 peppercorns

8 whole cloves

1 bay leaf

Kosher salt, if using fresh brisket

2 medium turnips, peeled and quartered

4 red new potatoes, peeled and quartered

3 large carrots, cut into thirds and thickest pieces quartered lengthwise

1 small head cabbage, cut into fourths

Horseradish sauce for serving

Mustard for serving

### DIRECTIONS

1. In a 5- or 6-quart Dutch oven, add brisket and cover with an inch of water. Add peppercorns, cloves, and bay leaf to the pot and bring to a boil. If using fresh brisket, add 1 teaspoon salt for every quart of water.

2. Bring to a simmer and then cover, lowering heat until it is barely simmering. Keep at a low simmer for 4 hours or until meat is tender (a fork goes through easily).

3. Remove meat and set aside, keeping warm. Add turnips, potatoes, carrots, and cabbage to the pot. Check broth for taste. If it is too salty, add a little more water to taste.

# NORTHEAST MENU

4. Raise the temperature and bring soup to a high simmer. Cook at a high simmer until done, about 15 to 30 minutes longer, depending on the size of your cut vegetables.

5. Slice meat in thin slices across the grain. Serve in bowls, a few pieces of meat in each; add vegetables and broth to each bowl. Serve with horseradish sauce, mustard, or both.

# NORTHEAST MENU

## Mini Whoopie Pies

**LEVEL 2**

*Makes 24 pies*

### INGREDIENTS

2¼ cups all-purpose flour
½ cup unsweetened cocoa powder
1 teaspoon baking soda
2 teaspoons cream of tartar
1 teaspoon salt
⅔ cup vegetable shortening
1¼ cups granulated sugar
2 large eggs
3 teaspoons vanilla extract
1 cup milk
½ cup unsalted butter
1 cup confectioners' sugar
2 cups marshmallow creme

### DIRECTIONS

1. Preheat oven to 350°F. Grease 2 large baking sheets; set aside.
2. In a medium bowl, whisk together flour, cocoa, baking soda, cream of tartar, and salt; set aside.
3. In a large bowl, cream together shortening and granulated sugar. Beat in eggs and 2 teaspoons vanilla extract. Alternately add flour mixture and milk, beating until fully combined.
4. Drop dough by tablespoons 2 inches apart onto prepared baking sheets.

# NORTHEAST MENU

5. Bake for 8 to 10 minutes or until darker around the edges and firm to the touch. Transfer cakes to a wire rack to cool completely.

6. In a medium bowl, beat together butter and confectioners' sugar. Beat in marshmallow creme and remaining teaspoon vanilla extract until smooth.

7. Spoon 1 tablespoon filling onto bottom of a cake. Press bottom of a second cake against filling to make a sandwich. Repeat with remaining cakes and filling.

8. To store, layer whoopie pies between sheets of waxed paper in an airtight container and refrigerate for up to 2 days.

# SOUTHEAST MENU

## Creamy Coleslaw

**LEVEL 1**

*Serves 6*

### INGREDIENTS

1 small head green cabbage, quartered, cored, and thinly sliced or shredded

2 large carrots, shredded

1 cup mayonnaise

1½ tablespoons sugar

1 teaspoon celery seed

3 tablespoons white vinegar

1 teaspoon lemon juice

Salt and pepper, to taste

### DIRECTIONS

1. In a large bowl, toss cabbage and carrots to combine.
2. In a medium bowl, prepare dressing: whisk and combine mayonnaise, sugar, celery seed, vinegar, lemon juice, salt, and pepper.
3. Pour dressing over cabbage mixture and stir to coat evenly. Cover and refrigerate 1 hour prior to serving.

# SOUTHEAST MENU

## Sweet and Easy Corn on the Cob

**LEVEL 1**

*Serves 6*

### INGREDIENTS

2 tablespoons sugar

1 tablespoon lemon juice

6 ears of corn on the cob, husks and silks removed

### DIRECTIONS

1. Fill a large pot about three-quarters full of water and bring to a boil.
2. Stir in sugar and lemon juice, dissolving sugar.
3. Gently place ears of corn into boiling water, cover the pot, turn off the heat, and let corn cook in hot water until tender, about 10 minutes.
4. Using tongs, carefully remove ears of corn from the pot.

# SOUTHEAST MENU

## Southern Fried Chicken

**LEVEL 3**

*Serves 4*

### INGREDIENTS

1½ cups milk
2 large eggs
2½ cups all-purpose flour
2 tablespoons salt,
    plus additional for sprinkling
2 teaspoons black pepper
4 pounds bone-in, skin-on chicken pieces
Vegetable oil for frying

### DIRECTIONS

1. Preheat oven to 200°F and place a rack in a large baking pan.
2. In a medium bowl, combine milk and eggs. Whisk to blend well.
3. In a large, heavy-duty resealable plastic food storage bag, combine flour, salt, and pepper. Seal and shake to combine.
4. Dip chicken pieces in milk and egg mixture and let excess drip off into bowl. Set already dipped pieces aside on a plate until you have three or four.
5. Add dipped chicken pieces to bag of seasoned flour.
6. Seal bag and shake well to coat chicken pieces thoroughly.
7. Remove to a plate and repeat with remaining chicken pieces.
8. Heat oil in a deep, heavy skillet to 350°F. While it's heating up, line a large serving plate with paper towels and set aside.

9. Fry chicken a few pieces at a time for about 10 minutes on each side, or until golden brown and thoroughly cooked. Be careful not to put too many pieces in at once—even if they comfortably fit—since doing so will dramatically drop the oil's temperature, affecting the crispness of the final product. Note that chicken breasts will take a little less time to fry than dark meat pieces.

10. With a slotted spoon, move done chicken pieces onto paper towel–lined platter to drain. Sprinkle immediately with salt.

11. Transfer drained and seasoned chicken to prepared pan with a rack. Keep warm in preheated oven while frying subsequent batches. Depending on the size of your pan, this recipe will require about 3 to 4 batches.

# SOUTHEAST MENU

## Key Lime Pie

**LEVEL 2**

*Serves 8*

### INGREDIENTS

1½ cups graham cracker crumbs
¼ cup sugar
½ teaspoon cinnamon
½ cup butter, melted
One 14-ounce can sweetened condensed milk

3 egg yolks
½ cup fresh squeezed key lime juice
Whipped cream for serving
Lime slices for garnish

### DIRECTIONS

1. Preheat oven to 350°F.
2. In a medium bowl, combine graham cracker crumbs, sugar, and cinnamon and mix together until well combined.
3. Add melted butter and stir until mixture resembles wet sand.
4. Press into a 9-inch pie pan and bake 6–8 minutes.
5. Remove from oven and cool.
6. In a large bowl, combine sweetened condensed milk and egg yolks; whisk until smooth.
7. Add key lime juice and whisk until smooth.
8. Pour filling into pie crust and bake at 350°F for 10 minutes.
9. Cool on a wire rack for 1 hour.
10. Chill pie in the refrigerator 4 hours or overnight.
11. Top with whipped cream and garnish with lime slices.

# MIDWEST
## M·E·N·U

 Wisconsin Cheese Soup
Broccoli Casserole
Scalloped Potatoes
Meatloaf
Cherry Pie

# MIDWEST MENU

## Wisconsin Cheese Soup

**LEVEL 2**

*Makes 4 (1-cup) servings*

### INGREDIENTS

3½ cups chicken broth
½ cup chopped carrot
1 small onion, chopped
1 rib celery, chopped
½ cup milk
20 ounces American cheese, roughly chopped
4 drops hot pepper sauce (or less if you don't want heat)
⅓ cup all-purpose flour

### DIRECTIONS

1. In a 4-quart saucepan, add 1 cup chicken broth, carrot, onion, and celery.
2. Cook over medium-high heat 8 to 10 minutes or until onion is softened.
3. Add 2 cups chicken broth, milk, cheese, and hot pepper sauce (if using). Reduce heat to medium; cook 5 to 8 minutes or until cheese is melted.
4. In a medium bowl, add flour and stir in remaining chicken broth until smooth. Stir flour mixture into soup. Cook, stirring constantly, 1 to 2 minutes or until soup is slightly thickened.

# MIDWEST MENU

## Broccoli Casserole

**LEVEL 1**

*Serves 8*

### INGREDIENTS

One 10-ounce package frozen broccoli, cooked and drained

1 cup mayonnaise

1 cup sharp cheddar cheese, grated

One 10.75-ounce can condensed cream of mushroom soup

2 eggs, lightly beaten

2 cups saltine crackers, crushed

2 tablespoons unsalted butter, melted

### DIRECTIONS

1. Preheat oven to 350°F. Spray a 13 × 9-inch baking dish with nonstick spray.
2. In a large bowl, combine broccoli, mayonnaise, cheese, soup, and eggs. Mix well.
3. Pour mixture into prepared baking dish. Top with crushed crackers and pour melted butter over crackers.
4. Bake for 35 minutes or until set and browned.

# MIDWEST MENU

## Scalloped Potatoes

**LEVEL 2**

*Serves 8 to 10*

### INGREDIENTS

4 pounds Yukon gold potatoes, thinly sliced

2 teaspoons kosher salt

1 teaspoon ground black pepper

1 cup shredded Parmesan cheese

1 cup shredded cheddar cheese

½ cup heavy whipping cream

Chopped fresh chives for garnish

### DIRECTIONS

1. Preheat oven to 400°F. Spray a 13 × 9-inch baking dish with nonstick spray.

2. Arrange one-third of potato slices in bottom of prepared pan. Sprinkle potatoes with ½ teaspoon salt, ¼ teaspoon pepper, and ¼ cup each Parmesan and cheddar. Repeat layers twice. Drizzle cream onto potatoes. Top with remaining salt, pepper, and cheeses.

3. Bake until potatoes are tender and top is golden brown, about 1 hour. Let stand for 5 minutes before serving. Garnish with chives, if desired.

# MIDWEST MENU

## Meatloaf

**LEVEL 2**
Serves 4

**TIP** Replace ground beef with ground turkey.

### INGREDIENTS

1 pound extra-lean ground beef
½ cup yellow onion, chopped
½ cup green pepper, chopped
1 large egg, lightly beaten
One 14.5-ounce can diced tomatoes, drained
½ cup Parmesan cheese, grated

1 teaspoon salt
½ teaspoon black pepper
1 teaspoon olive oil
1 large Vidalia onion, sliced in half and cut into ¼-inch slices
1½ tablespoons Dijon mustard

### DIRECTIONS

1. Preheat oven to 375°F.
2. In a large bowl, combine beef, yellow onion, green pepper, egg, diced tomatoes, Parmesan, salt, and black pepper. Mix well.
3. Place mixture in a large baking dish, shaping meat into a 3 × 8-inch loaf, and bake for 30 minutes.
4. Caramelize onions. In a large skillet, heat olive oil over medium heat and add Vidalia onion. Cook while stirring until onion slices soften. Continue cooking and stirring until onions are golden brown, approximately an additional 15 minutes.
5. Remove meatloaf from oven and spread mustard over top. Sprinkle caramelized onions on top, return meatloaf to oven, and continue baking for 15 minutes until meatloaf is browned. An adult should check with a meat thermometer to be sure the temperature registers 155–160°F. Remove from oven and let sit 5 minutes prior to slicing and serving.

# MIDWEST MENU

## Cherry Pie

**LEVEL 2**

*Serves 8*

### INGREDIENTS

1 cup plus 1 tablespoon sugar
3 tablespoons cornstarch
¼ teaspoon salt
⅔ cup cherry juice
Two 2½-pound bags frozen sour cherries

½ teaspoon almond extract
2 tablespoons butter
Pastry for double-crust 9-inch pie
2 teaspoons milk

### DIRECTIONS

1. Preheat oven to 400°F.
2. In a large saucepan, combine 1 cup sugar, cornstarch, and salt, stirring to remove lumps. Stir cherry juice into sugar mixture. Cook over medium heat until smooth, stirring constantly. Add cherries. Simmer until liquid is thickened and transparent, about 4 minutes. Stir once or twice. Add almond extract and butter, stirring until butter melts. Allow mixture to cool.
3. On a lightly floured sheet of waxed paper, roll half of pastry to ⅛-inch thickness. Place in a 9-inch deep-dish pie plate; trim off excess pastry along edges. Pour cooled cherry mixture into pastry shell.
4. Roll remaining pastry to ⅛-inch thickness; cut into strips, if you want to make a lattice-topped pie. Otherwise, transfer entire pastry to top of pie. Trim off excess pastry along edges and cut slits in top crust for steam to escape.
5. Brush top of pastry shell lightly with milk or cream, and sprinkle pastry with 1 tablespoon sugar.
6. Bake for 55 minutes or until golden brown.

# SOUTHWEST MENU

## Guacamole

**LEVEL 1**

*Makes 2 cups*

### INGREDIENTS

2 ripe avocados
½ teaspoon salt
1 garlic clove, finely minced
1 teaspoon fresh lime juice or to taste
1 medium-sized tomato, chopped
¼ cup red onion, finely chopped
1 medium-size jalapeño, minced
2 tablespoons fresh cilantro, coarsely chopped

### DIRECTIONS

1. Halve and pit the avocados and scoop pulp into a medium bowl.
2. Add salt and garlic; add lime juice to taste.
3. Fold in tomato, onion, chile and cilantro. Let stand a few minutes before serving to allow flavors to blend. Taste and adjust seasonings as necessary.

# SOUTHWEST MENU

## Southwestern Rice

**LEVEL 2**

*Serves 8*

### INGREDIENTS

1 tablespoon olive oil
1 green pepper, diced
1 onion, chopped
2 garlic cloves, minced
1 cup uncooked long-grain rice
½ teaspoon ground cumin
⅛ teaspoon ground turmeric
One 14.5-ounce can chicken broth
2 cups frozen corn, thawed
One 15-ounce can black beans, rinsed and drained
One 10-ounce can diced tomatoes with green chiles, undrained

### DIRECTIONS

1. In a large skillet, heat oil over medium-high heat. Sauté pepper and onion, and add garlic; cook and stir for 1 minute.

2. Stir in rice, cumin, turmeric, and broth and bring to a boil. Reduce heat; simmer, covered, until rice is tender, about 15 minutes.

3. Stir in corn, beans, and tomatoes with chiles. Cook, covered, until heated through.

# SOUTHWEST MENU

## Chicken Enchiladas

**LEVEL 2**

*Serves 8*

### INGREDIENTS

1 tablespoon olive oil

1 cup onions, chopped

2 cloves garlic, minced

2 cups cooked chicken, shredded

One 15-ounce can black beans, rinsed

4 ounces green chiles, diced

1 teaspoon chili powder

1 teaspoon ground cumin

½ teaspoon dried oregano

½ teaspoon salt

1¼ cups enchilada sauce (see recipe)

3 cups Mexican shredded cheese

8 large flour tortillas

### DIRECTIONS

1. Preheat oven to 350°F. Grease a 9 × 13-inch baking pan.
2. In a large skillet, heat olive oil over medium heat. Add onions and cook until softened, approximately 3 minutes. Add garlic, stirring for less than a minute. Turn off heat.
3. Add chicken, beans, chiles, chili powder, cumin, oregano, salt, and ½ cup enchilada sauce to the skillet. Stir until combined.
4. Spread ½ cup enchilada sauce over bottom of prepared baking pan.
5. In the middle of a tortilla, place ½ cup chicken and bean mixture and top with ⅓ cup cheese. Tightly roll up filled tortilla and place seam side down in prepared baking pan. Repeat until all eight tortillas are filled and placed in pan.
6. Spread remaining enchilada sauce over top of enchiladas and sprinkle with remaining cheese. Bake enchiladas for 20 to 25 minutes, until hot and bubbly. Let rest for 5 minutes and serve with your choice of toppings (cilantro, onions, sour cream).

# SOUTHWEST MENU

## Enchilada Sauce

**LEVEL 1**

### INGREDIENTS

3 tablespoons flour (whole wheat flour, all-purpose flour, and gluten-free flour blends all work!)

1 tablespoon ground chili powder (optional, or reduce if sensitive to spice)

1 teaspoon ground cumin

½ teaspoon garlic powder

¼ teaspoon dried oregano

¼ teaspoon salt, to taste

Pinch of cinnamon (optional)

3 tablespoons olive oil

2 tablespoons tomato paste

2 cups vegetable broth

1 teaspoon apple cider vinegar or distilled white vinegar

Freshly ground black pepper, to taste

### DIRECTIONS

1. In a small bowl, mix together flour, chili powder (if using), cumin, garlic powder, oregano, salt, and cinnamon (if using).
2. In a medium pot over medium heat, warm oil until it's hot enough that a light sprinkle of flour and spice mixture sizzles on contact; this will take a few minutes.
3. Once oil is ready, pour in flour and spice mixture and whisk constantly until the color darkens, approximately 1 minute. Whisk tomato paste into mixture, and then slowly pour in broth while whisking to remove lumps.
4. Increase heat to medium-high and bring mixture to a simmer. Reduce heat and continue whisking for 5 to 7 minutes until sauce has thickened.
5. Remove from heat, whisk in vinegar, and season to taste with black pepper and more salt, to taste.

# SOUTHWEST MENU

## Mango Pineapple Sorbet with Honey

**LEVEL 2**

*Serves 2*

### INGREDIENTS

3 cups papaya nectar or orange juice
1⅔ cups frozen mango chunks
1⅔ cups pineapple chunks, canned or frozen
¾ cup honey
⅓ cup fresh lime juice

### DIRECTIONS

1. In a food processor, puree 1½ cups papaya nectar or orange juice, mango chunks, pineapple chunks, honey, and fresh lime juice. Stir in remaining 1½ cups papaya nectar or orange juice.

2. Pour mixture into 9-inch freezer-safe pan. Place in freezer for 3 to 6 hours or until firm.

3. Remove from freezer and transfer mixture to mixer bowl. Beat with an electric mixer until slushy but not thawed.

4. Return to pan and freeze for 2 to 4 hours or until firm.

5. Remove from freezer and scoop sorbet into small serving dishes.

# WEST MENU

## Country Potato Salad

**LEVEL 1**

*Serves 6*

### INGREDIENTS

6–8 medium Yukon Gold potatoes, peeled (about 2 pounds)

¼ cup red onion, chopped finely

3 stalks celery, chopped finely

3 eggs, hard boiled, chopped

#### DRESSING

1 cup mayonnaise

2 teaspoons yellow mustard

¼ cup sweet relish

1 teaspoon salt

½ teaspoon black pepper

½ teaspoon paprika, plus more for garnish if desired

### DIRECTIONS

1. Add potatoes to a large pot, cover with water (1 to 2 inches above potatoes), and cook until fork-tender.
2. Remove potatoes from pot, let cool for 10 minutes, and cut into 2-inch cubes.
3. In a large bowl, add chopped potatoes, onion, celery, and eggs.
4. In a small bowl, combine mayonnaise, mustard, relish, salt, pepper, and paprika and whisk until well combined.
5. Add dressing to potatoes and stir gently to combine.
6. Cover and store in refrigerator until ready to serve.

# WEST MENU

## Cowboy Dinner (Cornbread, Beef, and Bean Casserole)

**LEVEL 3**

*Serves 6 to 8*

### INGREDIENTS

**FILLING**

1½–2 pounds ground beef or turkey

1 cup yellow onion, diced

1 teaspoon salt

½ teaspoon black pepper

1 cup corn kernels, frozen

1½ cups salsa

One 15-ounce can black beans, rinsed and drained

1–2 cups cheddar cheese, shredded

**CORNBREAD TOPPING**

½ cup cornmeal

1½ cups flour

⅓ cup sugar

1 tablespoon baking powder

½ teaspoon salt

⅓ cup oil

2 large eggs

1¼ cups milk

### DIRECTIONS

1. Preheat oven to 375°F. Lightly grease a 9 × 13-inch pan and set aside.
2. In a large skillet over medium heat, cook ground beef, onion, salt, and pepper until meat is fully cooked. Drain grease from pan. Stir in corn, salsa, and beans.

# WEST MENU

3. Spread beef mixture evenly in prepared pan and set aside.

4. In a medium bowl, whisk together cornmeal, flour, sugar, baking powder, and salt. Make a well in the center and add oil, eggs, and milk. Whisk together until just combined.

5. Sprinkle cheese over beef mixture. Pour cornbread batter over the top and spread evenly all the way to the edges.

6. Bake for 40 to 45 minutes until cornbread is baked through. When a toothpick inserted in center comes out clean and cornbread top springs back when lightly touched, casserole is done. Remove from oven and let sit for 5 to 10 minutes prior to serving.

# WEST MENU

## Wyoming Cowboy Cookies

**LEVEL 2**

*Makes 12 cookies*

### INGREDIENTS

½ cup coconut, shredded
6 tablespoons pecans, chopped
½ cup butter, melted
¾ cup brown sugar
1 large egg
¾ teaspoon vanilla extract
1 cup all-purpose flour
½ teaspoon baking soda
¼ teaspoon sea salt
1 cup old-fashioned oats
1 cup chocolate chips

### DIRECTIONS

1. Preheat oven to 350°F. Line 2 baking sheets with parchment paper.
2. Place shredded coconut and pecans on a baking sheet and bake for 6 minutes or until toasted, moving around halfway through.
3. In a large bowl, using a mixer, cream butter and sugar until light and fluffy.
4. Add egg and vanilla extract and beat together.
5. In another bowl, combine flour, baking soda, and salt. Add this dry mixture to wet mixture and stir until well combined.
6. Stir in oats, chocolate chips, and toasted coconut and pecans.
7. Using an ice cream scooper, drop cookie batter onto baking sheets 2 inches apart. Bake for 12 minutes.

# RECIPES BY CATEGORY

## Drinks
Frozen Lemonade 29
Sunburst Drink 41

## Breakfast
Apple Cider Doughnuts 18
Avocado Toast 117
Blueberry Hazelnut Breakfast Cookies 134
Blueberry Muffins 86
Breakfast Burritos with Avocado-Tomato Salsa 103
Brown Sugar Oat Muffins 81
Buñelos Aga (Banana Doughnuts) 153
Denver Omelet 120
Egg and Sweet Corn Frittata 80
Honey Vanilla French Toast 92
Huckleberry Pop Tarts 124
Huevos Rancheros 106
Johnny Cakes 30
Oklahoma Cheese Grits 109
Pecan Pie Mini Muffins 37
Strawberry Smoothie 5
Wheat Cinnamon Rolls 127

## Salads/Soups
Cherry Salad 83
Cucumber Salad 154
Green Bean Salad 22
New Hampshire Corn Chowder 20
Pineapple Cucumber Lime Jell-O Salad 136
Senate Bean Soup 144
Shrimp Cocktail 133
Waldorf Salad 25
Wisconsin Cheese Soup 99

## Entrées
Authentic Cincinnati Chili 94
Baked Chicken Chimichangas 102
Beef Pasties 129
Cheeseburgers in Puff Pastry 3
Cheese Fondue 98
Chicago-Style Hot Dog 74
Chicago-Style Pizza 72
Chicken Enchiladas 186
Chicken-Fried Steak 108
Classic Pork Tenderloin Sandwiches 75

Classic Reuben Sandwiches 89

Corned Beef and Cabbage 166

Cowboy Dinner (Cornbread, Beef, and Bean Casserole) 191

Crab Cakes 11

Empanadillas (Puerto Rican Fried Turnovers) 146

Fish Tacos 118

Fried Ravioli 87

Frogmore Stew 59

Hot Brown Sandwiches 45

Lobster Rolls 8

Meatloaf 181

Minnesota Hot Dish Casserole 85

Nashville Hot Chicken 60

Ozark Sloppy Joes 88

Palusami 155

Pepperoni Rolls 66

Philly Cheesesteak 26

Salmon Croquettes 114

Shrimp and Grits 58

Slow Cooker Texas Pulled Pork 110

Southern Fried Chicken 43

Wyoming Stew 140

## Sides

Almond Butter and Nut Pear Wedges 135

Arkansas Rice Casserole 39

Boiled Peanuts 63

Boston Baked Beans 14

Broccoli Casserole 179

Callaloo 159

Coconut Rice 150

Corn Fritters 90

Country Potato Salad 111

Creamy Coleslaw 57

Emma's Applesauce 139

Enchilada Sauce 187

Fried Pickles 38

Fungi 157

Guacamole 105

Ham and Cheese Biscuits 64

Honey Butter 69

Idaho Fries 126

Macaroni and Cheese 32

Mambo Sauce 145

Mojo Verde 149

Onion Rings 132

Oven Fried Green Tomatoes 36

Oven-Roasted Vegetables 97

Pimento Cheese 55

Potato Casserole 137

Roasted Pineapple Salsa 122

Scalloped Potatoes 180

Skillet Cornbread 68

Sofrito 147

Southwestern Rice 185

Spam Fries 123

Sweet and Easy Corn on the Cob 79

Sweet Potato Balls 56

Tostones (Fried Green Plantains) 148

Wholesome Wheat Bread 82

Wild Mushroom Barley 138

## Dessert

Banana Pudding 62

Berger Cookies 12

Blueberry Meringue Pie 115

Buckeyes 93

Cherry Pie 84

Chippers (Chocolate-Covered Potato Chips) 91

Easy King Cake 48

Fondant 51

Kentucky Derby Pie 47

Key Lime Pie 40

Kuchen 96

Mango Pineapple Sorbet with Honey 188

Maple Candy 31

Mini Boston Cream Pie 1

Mini Whoopie Pies 9

Mississippi Mud Pie 52

No-Bake Peanut Butter Pie 42

Peach Pie 6

Red Velvet Cake 23

Rosketti 151

Salt Water Taffy 21

Samoan Poi 156

Soft Pretzels 27

Soft Pumpkin Cookies 2

Sugar Cream Pie 77

Watermelon Sorbet 121

Wyoming Cowboy Cookies 141

Yeti Baked Alaska 49

# RECIPES BY LEVEL OF DIFFICULTY

## Drinks
Frozen Lemonade 29
Sunburst Drink 41

## Breakfast
Avocado Toast 117
Blueberry Muffins 86
Pecan Pie Mini Muffins 37
Strawberry Smoothie 5

## Salads/Soups
Cherry Salad 83
Cucumber Salad 154
Green Bean Salad 22
Shrimp Cocktail 133
Waldorf Salad 25

## Entrées
Cheeseburgers in Puff Pastry 3
Cheese Fondue 98
Chicago-Style Hot Dog 74
Crab Cakes 11
Minnesota Hot Dish Casserole 85
Slow Cooker Texas Pulled Pork 110

## Sides
Almond Butter and Nut Pear Wedges 135
Arkansas Rice Casserole 39
Boiled Peanuts 63
Broccoli Casserole 179
Coconut Rice 150
Country Potato Salad 111

Creamy Coleslaw 57

Emma's Applesauce 139

Enchilada Sauce 187

Guacamole 105

Honey Butter 69

Idaho Fries 126

Mambo Sauce 145

Mojo Verde 149

Oven Fried Green Tomatoes 36

Pimento Cheese 55

Potato Casserole 137

Sofrito 147

Sweet and Easy Corn on the Cob 79

## Dessert

Chippers (Chocolate-Covered Potato Chips) 91

Easy King Cake 48

Fondant 51

Maple Candy 31

No-Bake Peanut Butter Pie 42

Watermelon Sorbet 121

## Breakfast

Blueberry Hazelnut Breakfast Cookies 134

Brown Sugar Oat Muffins 81

Denver Omelet 120

Egg and Sweet Corn Frittata 80

Honey Vanilla French Toast 92

Johnny Cakes 30

Oklahoma Cheese Grits 109

## Salads/Soups

New Hampshire Corn Chowder 20

Pineapple Cucumber Lime Jell-O Salad 136

Senate Bean Soup 144

Wisconsin Cheese Soup 99

## Entrées

Authentic Cincinnati Chili 94

Chicago-Style Pizza 72

Chicken Enchiladas 186

Classic Reuben Sandwiches 89

Corned Beef and Cabbage 166

Fish Tacos 118

Fried Ravioli 87

Frogmore Stew 59

Hot Brown Sandwiches 45

Lobster Rolls 8

Meatloaf 181

Ozark Sloppy Joes 88

Philly Cheesesteak 26

Salmon Croquettes 114

Scalloped Potatoes 180

Shrimp and Grits 58

Wyoming Stew 140

RECIPES BY LEVEL OF DIFFICULTY 201

## Sides

Boston Baked Beans 14

Callaloo 159

Corn Fritters 90

Fried Pickles 38

Macaroni and Cheese 32

Oven-Roasted Vegetables 97

Roasted Pineapple Salsa 122

Skillet Cornbread 68

Southwestern Rice 185

Sweet Potato Balls 56

Wholesome Wheat Bread 82

Wild Mushroom Barley 138

## Dessert

Banana Pudding 62

Berger Cookies 12

Buckeyes 93

Cherry Pie 84

Kentucky Derby Pie 47

Key Lime Pie 40

Kuchen 96

Mango Pineapple Sorbet with Honey 188

Mini Whoopie Pies 9

Peach Pie 6

Rosketti 151

Salt Water Taffy 21

Samoan Poi 156

Soft Pretzels 27

Soft Pumpkin Cookies 2

Wyoming Cowboy Cookies 141

## Breakfast

Apple Cider Doughnuts 18

Breakfast Burritos with Avocado-Tomato Salsa 103

Buñelos Aga (Banana Doughnuts) 153

Huckleberry Pop Tarts 124

Huevos Rancheros 106

Wheat Cinnamon Rolls 127

## Entrées

Baked Chicken Chimichangas 102

Beef Pasties 129

Chicken-Fried Steak 108

Classic Pork Tenderloin Sandwiches 75

Cowboy Dinner (Cornbread, Beef, and Bean Casserole) 191

Empanadillas (Puerto Rican Fried Turnovers) 146

Nashville Hot Chicken 60

Palusami 155

Pepperoni Rolls 66

Southern Fried Chicken 43

## Sides

Fungi 157

Ham and Cheese Biscuits 64

Onion Rings 132

Spam Fries 123

Tostones (Fried Green Plantains) 148

## Dessert

Blueberry Meringue Pie 115

Mini Boston Cream Pie 15

Mississippi Mud Pie 52

Red Velvet Cake 23

Sugar Cream Pie 77

Yeti Baked Alaska 49

## Acknowledgments

Thank you to my dear friend P.J., whose love and support knows no bounds. You motivate me, challenge me, and are always there for me. Life is never dull when you are around. This book is a collaboration of our love and friendship.

Thank you to my family and friends, who stood by me when my world turned upside down. I am so grateful to have you by my side. I love you all. Nothing in life is guaranteed, so shoot for the stars.

This book could not have happened if it was not for P.J. Tierney and her incredible team at Kitchen Ink. Thank you for your time and invaluable insights and suggestions. Kate, there are not enough words to thank you for the illustrations. Your creativity and fortitude as we collaborated on getting the food just right were truly astonishing. I am grateful to Deb Murray, recipe creator extraordinaire—the Yeti is by far the best! Thanks to the crew at Wilsted & Taylor Publishing Services: Christine Taylor, LeRoy Wilsted, Nancy Koerner, Melody Lacina, Nancy Evans, Sophia Fox, and Evan Winslow Smith. Your hard work, patience, and dedication to a first-time creator are appreciated more than you will ever know.

I thank all the children I have had the pleasure of working with. You have enriched my life with your smiles, strength, and determination to make this world a better place. My hope for you is that your road trip through life is paved with love, laughter, and delicious food.

# INDEX

accordions, 99
Alabama, 35, 36–37
alarm clocks, 20
Alaska, 113, 114–16
Albuquerque, NM, 105
Alciatore, Antoine, 49
Aldrin, Buzz, 37
Almond Butter and Nut Pear Wedges, 135
aloha, 123
American Samoa, 143, 155–56
Andrews Church, Grafton, WV, 67
animal cookie joke, 55
Antoine's, New Orleans, LA, 49
Apple Cider Doughnuts, 18–19
apples, 98
    Emma's Applesauce, 139
    Waldorf Salad, 25, 164
Arizona, 101, 102–4
Arkansas, 35, 38–39
Arkansas Rice Casserole, 39
Armstrong, Neil, 37
Assateague Island, MD, 13
astronauts, 37
Authentic Cincinnati Chili, 94–95

avocados
    Avocado Toast, 117
    Breakfast Burritos with Avocado-Tomato Salsa, 103–4
    Guacamole, 105, 184

bacon, 3–4
    Boston Baked Beans, 14, 165
    Hot Brown Sandwiches, 45–46
    Shrimp and Grits, 58
Baked Alaska
    origins, 49
    Yeti Baked Alaska, 49–50
Baked Chicken Chimichangas, 102
bananas
    Banana Doughnuts (Buñelos Aga), 153
    Banana Pudding, 62
    Samoan Poi, 156
barbecue sauce
    Slow Cooker Texas Pulled Pork, 110
barley
    Wild Mushroom Barley, 138
baseball, 22
bats, 111

beans
- Boston Baked Beans, 14, 165
- Chicken Enchiladas, 186–87
- Cowboy Dinner (Cornbread, Beef, and Bean Casserole), 191–92
- Senate Bean Soup, 144
- Southwestern Rice, 185

beef
- Authentic Cincinnati Chili, 94–95
- Beef Pasties, 129–31
- Cheeseburgers in Puff Pastry, 3–4
- Chicken-Fried Steak, 108
- Cowboy Dinner (Cornbread, Beef, and Bean Casserole), 191–92
- Empanadillas (Puerto Rican Fried Turnovers), 146–47
- Meatloaf, 181
- Minnesota Hot Dish Casserole, 85
- Ozark Sloppy Joes, 88
- Palusami, 155
- Philly Cheesesteak, 26
- Wyoming Stew, 140
- *See also* corned beef

bell peppers, 120, 146, 147, 159
Ben & Jerry's, 33
Berger Cookies, 12–13

biscuits
- Ham and Cheese Biscuits, 64–65

blueberries
- Blueberry Hazelnut Breakfast Cookies, 134
- Blueberry Meringue Pie, 115–16
- Blueberry Muffins, 86

blue jeans, invention of, 133
Boiled Peanuts, 63
Boise State Broncos, 125
Boston Baked Beans, 14, 165
Boston Cream Pie, Mini, 15–17
Bracken Cave, San Antonio, TX, 111
Bread, Wholesome Wheat, 82
Breakfast Burritos with Avocado-Tomato Salsa, 103–4
Broccoli Casserole, 179
Brown Sugar Oat Muffins, 81
Buckeyes, 93
buffalo joke, 140
Buñelos Aga (Banana Doughnuts), 153

burgers
- Cheeseburgers in Puff Pastry, 3–4
- jokes, 4, 85

burritos
- Breakfast Burritos with Avocado-Tomato Salsa, 103–4
- joke, 102

Butter, Honey, 69

buttermilk
- substitute for, 36
- substituting with, 43

cabbage
- Corned Beef and Cabbage, 166–67
- Creamy Coleslaw, 57, 172
- joke, 25

cakes
- Easy King Cake, 48
- joke, 51
- Mini Boston Cream Pie, 15–17
- Red Velvet Cake, 23–24
- Yeti Baked Alaska, 49–50

California, 113, 117–19
Callaloo, 159
Carnival (festival), 158
chard, 155
Chattanooga, TN, 61
cheese
- Cheeseburgers in Puff Pastry, 3–4
- Cheese Fondue, 98
- Chicken Enchiladas, 186–87
- Ham and Cheese Biscuits, 64–65
- jokes, 99, 105
- Macaroni and Cheese, 32–33
- Oklahoma Cheese Grits, 109
- Philly Cheesesteak, 26
- Pimento Cheese, 55
- Wisconsin Cheese Soup, 99, 178

cherries
- Cherry Pie, 84, 182
- Cherry Salad, 83

Chicago, IL, 73
Chicago-Style Hot Dog, 74
Chicago-Style Pizza, 72–73
chicken
- Baked Chicken Chimichangas, 102
- Chicken Enchiladas, 186–87
- Nashville Hot Chicken, 60–61
- Southern Fried Chicken, 43–44, 174–75

Chicken-Fried Steak, 108
chicken soup, cream of
- Potato Casserole, 137
- Wyoming Stew, 140

Chili, Authentic Cincinnati, 94–95
Chincoteague ponies, 13
chocolate/chocolate chips
- Berger Cookies, 12–13
- Buckeyes, 93
- Chippers (Chocolate-Covered Potato Chips), 91
- Mini Whoopie Pies, 9–10, 168–69
- Mississippi Mud Pie, 52–54
- Wyoming Cowboy Cookies, 141, 193

cilantro, 122, 147
- Mojo Verde, 149

cinnamon rolls
- Easy King Cake, 48
- Wheat Cinnamon Rolls, 127–28

Classic Pork Tenderloin Sandwiches, 75–76
Classic Reuben Sandwiches, 89
Clayton, Don, 57
Cocktail Sauce, 133
cocoa powder, 9–10, 12
coconut
- Coconut Rice, 150
- Fungi, 157–58
- Wyoming Cowboy Cookies, 141, 193

coconut cream or milk
    Coconut Rice, 150
    Samoan Poi, 156
Coleslaw, Creamy, 57, 172
Collins, Michael, 37
Colorado, 113, 120–21
Concord, NH, 20
Connecticut, 1, 2–4
cookies
    Berger Cookies, 12–13
    Blueberry Hazelnut Breakfast Cookies, 134
    Rosketti, 151–52
    Soft Pumpkin Cookies, 2
    Wyoming Cowboy Cookies, 141, 193
corn
    Corn Fritters, 90
    Corn Palace, Mitchell, SD, 97
    Egg and Sweet Corn Frittata, 80
    New Hampshire Corn Chowder, 20
    Southwestern Rice, 185
    Sweet and Easy Corn on the Cob, 79, 173
corned beef
    Classic Reuben Sandwiches, 89
    Corned Beef and Cabbage, 166–67
cornmeal
    Cowboy Dinner (Cornbread, Beef, and Bean Casserole), 191–92
    Fungi, 157–58
    Johnny Cakes, 30
    Skillet Cornbread, 68
Corn Palace, Mitchell, SD, 97
Country Potato Salad, 111, 190
cowboys
    Cowboy Dinner (Cornbread, Beef, and Bean Casserole), 191–92
    joke, 128
    Wyoming Cowboy Cookies, 141, 193
crab
    Crab Cakes, 11
    horseshoe, 7
cream cheese
    Pimento Cheese, 55
Creamy Coleslaw, 57, 172
cucumbers
    Cucumber Salad, 154
    Pineapple Cucumber Lime Jell-O Salad, 136

Davis, Jacob, 133
Delaware, 1, 5–7
Denver Omelet, 120
Detroit, MI, 83
dinosaurs, 121
doctor joke, 153
doughnuts
    Apple Cider Doughnuts, 18–19
    Buñelos Aga (Banana Doughnuts), 153
Doumar, Abe, 88

Easy King Cake, 48
eggs, 92, 111, 190
    Denver Omelet, 120
    Egg and Sweet Corn Frittata, 80
    Huevos Rancheros, 106–7
    joke, 97
El Yunque National Forest, Puerto Rico, 146
Emma's Applesauce, 139
Empanadillas (Puerto Rican Fried Turnovers), 146–47
Enchiladas, Chicken, 186–87
Enchilada Sauce, 187

Fayetteville, NC, 57
fiddles, 39
Fish Tacos, 118–19
flag, Ohio, 94
Florida, 35, 40–41
Fondant, 51
fondue, 98
football, 125
Fort Keogh, MT, 131
French Toast, Honey Vanilla, 92
Fried Green Plantains (Tostones), 148–49
Fried Pickles, 38
Fried Ravioli, 87
Frogmore Stew, 59
Frozen Lemonade, 29
Fungi, 157–58

Georgia, 35, 42–44
Gobbler's Knob, PA, 28
Goldman, Sylvan, 109
graham crackers, 40, 176
Green Bean Salad, 22
grits
    Oklahoma Cheese Grits, 109
    Shrimp and Grits, 58
Groundhog Day, 28
Guacamole, 105, 184
Guam, 143, 153–54

ham
    Denver Omelet, 120
    Ham and Cheese Biscuits, 64–65
    Senate Bean Soup, 144
"Happy Birthday Song," 46
hash browns
    Potato Casserole, 137
Hawaii, 113, 122–23
Hawkeye Circus, IA, 80
hazelnuts
    Blueberry Hazelnut Breakfast Cookies, 134
Hill, Mildred and Patty Smith, 46
hogs, 33
Holmes, Ernest, 61
honey, 92
    Honey Butter, 69
    Honey Vanilla French Toast, 92

Mango Pineapple Sorbet with
    Honey, 188
horses, 13, 47
horseshoe crabs, 7
hot-air balloon festival, 105
Hot Brown Sandwiches, 45–46
hot dogs
    Chicago-Style Hot Dog, 74
Huckleberry Pop Tarts, 124–25
Huevos Rancheros, 106–7
Hutchins, Levi, 20

icing, fondant, 51
Idaho, 113, 124–26
Idaho Fries, 126
Illinois, 71, 72–74
Indiana, 71, 75–78
Iowa, 71, 79–80

jalapeño peppers, 105, 122, 147, 184
Jell-O
    Pineapple Cucumber Lime Jell-O
    Salad, 136
Johnny Cakes, 30
jokes, 4, 6, 8, 11, 15, 22, 25, 30, 31, 37, 39, 40, 42, 47, 51, 55, 56, 58, 62, 68, 72, 78, 79, 82, 85, 87, 90, 92, 95, 97, 99, 102, 105, 108, 110, 116, 118, 121, 122, 126, 128, 133, 135, 137, 139, 140, 144, 149, 153, 156, 158
Judson, Whitcomb L., 73

Kansas, 71, 81–82
Kentucky, 35, 45–47
Kentucky Derby Pie, 47
ketchup
    first recipe for, 65
    joke, 37
    Mambo Sauce, 145
Key Lime Pie, 40, 176
ko'ko' bird, 154
Kuchen, 96

Labadie's Bakery, Lewiston, ME, 9
Lassen, Louis, 3
lemons
    Frozen Lemonade, 29
    joke, 30
lime
    Key Lime Pie, 40, 176
    Pineapple Cucumber Lime Jell-O
    Salad, 136
Lobster Rolls, 8
Longview, WA, 138
Louie's Lunch, New Haven, CT, 3
Louisiana, 35, 48–51
Louisville, KY, 46

Macaroni and Cheese, 32–33
Maine, 1, 8–10
Mambo Sauce, 145
Mango Pineapple Sorbet with
    Honey, 188
Maple Candy, 31

marshmallow creme
    Fondant, 51
    Mini Whoopie Pies, 9–10, 168–69
Maryland, 1, 11–13
Massachusetts, 1, 14–17
Meatloaf, 181
melon joke, 121
meringue, 49–50, 115–16
Michigan, 71, 83–84
Midwest, 71–99, 178–82
Mini Whoopie Pies, 9–10, 168–69
Minnesota, 71, 85–86
Minnesota Hot Dish Casserole, 85
Mississippi, 35, 52–55
Mississippi Mud Pie, 52–54
Mississippi River, 54
Missouri, 71, 87–88
Mitchell, SD, 97
Mojo Verde, 149
monkeys, 59
Montana, 113, 127–31
moon landing, 37
Moon's Lake House, Saratoga Springs, NY, 25
Morgan Island, SC, 59
Mother's Day, 67
muffins
    Blueberry Muffins, 86
    Brown Sugar Oat Muffins, 81
    joke, 82
    Pecan Pie Mini Muffins, 37

mushrooms
    Arkansas Rice Casserole, 39
    Chicago-Style Pizza, 72–73
    Wild Mushroom Barley, 138
mushroom soup, cream of
    Broccoli Casserole, 179
    Minnesota Hot Dish Casserole, 85

NASA, Huntsville, AL, 37
Nashville Hot Chicken, 60–61
National Museum of Roller Skating, Lincoln, NE, 90
Nebraska, 71, 89–90
Nevada, 113, 132–33
New Hampshire, 1, 18–20
New Hampshire Corn Chowder, 20
New Jersey, 1, 21–22
New Mexico, 101, 105–7
New York, 1, 23–25
Nissen, George, 80
No-Bake Peanut Butter Pie, 42
North Carolina, 35, 56–57
North Dakota, 71, 91–92
Northeast, 1–33, 164–69
Northern Mariana Islands, 143, 150–52
nuts
    Almond Butter and Nut Pear Wedges, 135
    Blueberry Hazelnut Breakfast Cookies, 134
    Waldorf Salad, 25, 164
    *See also* peanuts; pecans

oats
- Blueberry Hazelnut Breakfast Cookies, 134
- Brown Sugar Oat Muffins, 81
- Wyoming Cowboy Cookies, 141, 193

ocean joke, 156
Ohio, 71, 93–95
Ojibwa, 54
Oklahoma, 101, 108–9
Oklahoma Cheese Grits, 109
okra
- Fungi, 157–58

olives, 146–47
Omni Parker House, Boston, MA, 16
Onion Rings, 132
orange juice, 188
- Mango Pineapple Sorbet with Honey, 188
- Sunburst Drink, 41

Oregon, 113, 134–35
Oreo cookies
- Mississippi Mud Pie, 52–54
- No-Bake Peanut Butter Pie, 42

Oven Fried Green Tomatoes, 36
Oven-Roasted Vegetables, 97
Ozark Sloppy Joes, 88

Palusami, 155
papaya nectar, 188
pasta, 94–95
- Fried Ravioli, 87
- Macaroni and Cheese, 32–33

peaches
- Kuchen, 96
- Peach Pie, 6–7

peanut butter
- Buckeyes, 93
- jokes, 42, 95
- No-Bake Peanut Butter Pie, 42

peanuts, 44
- Boiled Peanuts, 63

pears, 62
- Almond Butter and Nut Pear Wedges, 135

pecans
- Pecan Pie Mini Muffins, 37
- Wyoming Cowboy Cookies, 141, 193

Pennsylvania, 1, 26–28
pepperoni
- Chicago-Style Pizza, 72–73
- Pepperoni Rolls, 66–67

Peters, Amos, 138
Philly Cheesesteak, 26
Picket Wire Canyonlands, CO, 121
pickles
- Fried Pickles, 38
- joke, 39

pies
- Blueberry Meringue Pie, 115–16
- Cherry Pie, 84, 182
- history, 17
- jokes, 40, 78
- Kentucky Derby Pie, 47
- Key Lime Pie, 40, 176

212   INDEX

Mississippi Mud Pie, 52–54
No-Bake Peanut Butter Pie, 42
Peach Pie, 6–7
Sugar Cream Pie, 77–78
Pimento Cheese, 55
pineapple
  Mango Pineapple Sorbet with Honey, 188
  Pineapple Cucumber Lime Jell-O Salad, 136
  Roasted Pineapple Salsa, 122
pirate joke, 15
Pizza, Chicago-Style, 72–73
Plantains, Fried Green (Tostones), 148–49
polka, 99
Popcorn, IN (town), 76
Pop Tarts, Huckleberry, 124–25
pork
  Classic Pork Tenderloin Sandwiches, 75–76
  Ham and Cheese Biscuits, 64–65
  Slow Cooker Texas Pulled Pork, 110
  *See also* bacon; ham
Portland, OR, 135
potato chips
  Chippers (Chocolate-Covered Potato Chips), 91
  invention of, 25
potatoes
  Country Potato Salad, 111, 190
  Idaho Fries, 126
  joke, 90
  Oven-Roasted Vegetables, 97
  Potato Casserole, 137
  Salmon Croquettes, 114
  Scalloped Potatoes, 180
Pretzels, Soft, 27–28
Pudding, Banana, 62
Puerto Rican Fried Turnovers (Empanadillas), 146–47
Puerto Rico, 143, 146–49
Pumpkin Cookies, Soft, 2
Punxsutawney Phil, 28
putt-putt golf, 57

raisins, 25, 164
Ravioli, Fried, 87
Red Velvet Cake, 23–24
Redwood National and State Park forests, CA, 119
Reno, NV, 133
Rhode Island, 1, 29–30
rice
  Arkansas Rice Casserole, 39
  Coconut Rice, 150
  Southwestern Rice, 185
Roasted Pineapple Salsa, 122
roller skates, 90
Roosevelt, Theodore, 145
Rosketti, 151–52

salmon
  joke, 116
  Salmon Croquettes, 114

INDEX  213

saltine crackers
    Broccoli Casserole, 179
    Classic Pork Tenderloin Sandwiches, 75–76
Salt Water Taffy, 21
Samoan Poi, 156
sauerkraut, 89
Scalloped Potatoes, 180
Senate Bean Soup, 144
shopping carts, 109
shrimp
    Shrimp and Grits, 58
    Shrimp Cocktail, 133
Skillet Cornbread, 68
Slow Cooker Texas Pulled Pork, 110
Smoothie, Strawberry, 5
snowflake, largest, 131
soda pop, 83
Sofrito, 147
Soft Pretzels, 27–28
Soft Pumpkin Cookies, 2
sorbet
    Mango Pineapple Sorbet with Honey, 188
    Watermelon Sorbet, 121
soups
    joke, 144
    New Hampshire Corn Chowder, 20
    Senate Bean Soup, 144
    Wisconsin Cheese Soup, 99, 178
South Carolina, 35, 58–59
South Dakota, 71, 96–97

Southeast, 35–69, 172–76
Southern Fried Chicken, 43–44, 174–75
Southwest, 101–11, 184–88
Southwestern Rice, 185
Spam Fries, 123
Speck, George, 25
spinach, 159
    Cherry Salad, 83
squirrel bridges, 138
St. Helena Island, SC, 59
St. Louis Fair, MO, 88
Strauss, Levi, 133
strawberries
    joke, 108
    Strawberry Smoothie, 5
Strite, Charles, 85
Sugar Cream Pie, 77–78
Sunburst Drink, 41
sunflowers, 92
Sweet and Easy Corn on the Cob, 79, 173
Sweet Potato Balls, 56

Tennessee, 35, 60–62
Texas, 101, 110–11
toast
    Avocado Toast, 117
    Honey Vanilla French Toast, 92
toaster, 85
tomatoes, 37
    Breakfast Burritos with Avocado-Tomato Salsa, 103–4

Oven Fried Green Tomatoes, 36
  Roasted Pineapple Salsa, 122
Tornado Alley, 81
tortillas
  Baked Chicken Chimichangas, 102
  Breakfast Burritos with Avocado-Tomato Salsa, 103–4
  Chicken Enchiladas, 186–87
  Fish Tacos, 118–19
  Huevos Rancheros, 106–7
Tostones (Fried Green Plantains), 148–49
tow truck, 61
trampoline, 80
tropical rainforest, 146
turkey, ground, 181, 191–92

US Virgin Islands, 143, 157–59
Utah, 113, 136–37

vegetables, roasted, 97
Vermont, 1, 31–33
Vernor's Ginger Ale, 83
Virginia, 35, 63–65
Virgin Islands, US, 143, 157–59
volcanoes, 152

waffle cone, 88
Waldorf Salad, 25, 164
Washington (state), 113, 138–39
Washington, D.C., 143, 144–45
Washington, George, 145
Waterbury, VT, 33
West, 113–14, 190–93
West Virginia, 35, 66–69
Wheat Cinnamon Rolls, 127–28
White House, 145
Wholesome Wheat Bread, 82
Whoopie Pies, Mini, 9–10, 168–69
Wild Mushroom Barley, 138
Wisconsin, 71, 98–99
Wisconsin Cheese Soup, 99, 178
World of Accordions (museum), WI, 99
World's Smallest Park, Portland, OR, 135
Wyoming, 113, 140–41
Wyoming Cowboy Cookies, 141, 193
Wyoming Stew, 140

Yeti Baked Alaska, 49–50
Yuma, AZ, 104

zippers, 73

INDEX 215

MAKE MEMORIES IN THE KITCHEN

# Books for Kids Who Love to Cook!

## HAMISH THE HEDGEHOG

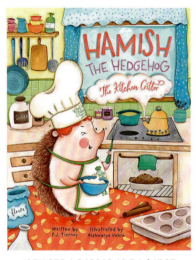

ISBN 978-1-943016-10-5 | $17.95

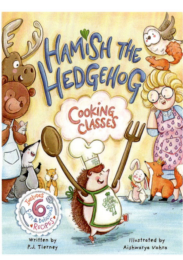

ISBN 978-1-943016-15-0 | $17.95

ISBN 978-1-943016-11-2 | $22.95

### Made with Love
#### Kid's Cookbook with Apron

Tie on this adorable apron and get cooking! The 80-page cookbook, which comes with an adjustable and machine-washable apron, illustrates 30 delicious, easy-to-follow recipes such as French Toast Sticks, Chicken Quesadillas, and Lemon Bars—all made with love.

### A new book series for kids who love to cook!

Follow the adventures of Hamish the Hedgehog and create six kid-friendly, parent-approved yummy recipes in this delightfully entertaining storybook cookbook series.

### Find the hidden cat in every book!

@KITCHENINKPUBLISHING
KITCHENINKPUBLISHING.COM

ON SALE NOW | WHEREVER BOOKS ARE SOLD